BLIND FAITH

**The Extraordinary Real-Life Story
Of A Woman From Liverpool, England,
Who Dared to Believe God And
Pioneered A Missionary Work
Among The Blind of Kano, Nigeria**

Anne Wooding
With
Dan Wooding

ASSIST BOOKS
PO Box 2126
Garden Grove, CA 92642-2126
In Cooperation with WinePress Publishing,
PO Box 1406, Mukilteo, WA 98275

To order additional copies of this book send $9.95 + $1.50 for shipping and handling (for each book) to:

ASSIST BOOKS
PO Box 2126
Garden Grove, CA 92642-2126

For quantity discounts, please call (714) 530-6598.

ACKNOWLEDGMENTS

I would like to express my heartfelt thanks to Michael Hylton for his invaluable help in preparing this book and also Sharon Hylton, who did a magnificent job in editing it. I would also like to thank my dear daughter-in-law, Norma Wooding, for doing the final proof reading of the book.

Anne Wooding
Liverpool, England

Some books by Dan Wooding

Junkies are People Too
Stresspoint
I Thought Terry Dene Was Dead
Exit The Devil (with Trevor Dearing)
Train of Teror (with Mini Loman)
Rick Wakeman, the Caped Crusader
King Squealer (with Maurice O'Mahoney)
Farewell Leicester Square (with Henry Hollis)
Uganda Holocaust (with Ray Barnett)
Miracles in Sin City (with Howard Cooper)
God's Smuggler to China (with Brother David and Sarah Bruce)
Prophets of Revolution (with Peter Asael Gonzales)
Brother Andrew
Guerilla for Christ (with Salu Daka Ndebele)
Million Dollar Promise (with Duane Logsdon)
Twenty-Six Lead Soldiers
Secret Missions
Singing In The Dark (with Barry Taylor)
Lost for Words (with Stuart Mill)
Let There Be Light (with Roger Oakland)
Rock Priest (with David Pierce)
He Intends Victory . . .
Russia, You Are Loved (with Hannu Haukka)
Return to the Hermit Kingdom (with Isaac Lee)

Some of these books are available from:
ASSIST, PO Box 2126,
Garden Grove, CA 92642-2126, USA
or phone: (714) 530-6598

FOREWORD

It wasn't just the Beatles that came from Liverpool, England. So did a committed young Christian woman called Anne Wooding who decided she wanted to take the "Long and Winding Road" in the 1930s from this bustling sea port on the River Mersey to teach the age-old message of love and salvation of faith in Jesus Christ to the physically and spiritually blind people of Nigeria, West Africa.

In this inspiring and challenging autobiography, co-authored with her son, Dan Wooding, who has been attending the church I pastor, Calvary Chapel of Costa Mesa, since June 1982, when he emigrated to the United States, you will read the moving story of how Anne went from the mean streets of Liverpool, to a missionary training college in London, to sailing from Liverpool to Lagos in the first steps of a true-life missionary adventure.

Before setting sail for a new life in Africa, Anne trained in the Braille language and then helped to pioneer an extraordinary work amongst the blind of the walled Muslim city of Kano in Northern Nigeria. She was the first white woman missionary allowed by the Emir (King) of Kano to work in that city.

It was while she was studying the Hausa language at the Sudan Interior Mission (SIM) language school that she met up with Alf Wooding, a diminutive young missionary with a large heart for missions and who also hailed from Liverpool. They eventually fell in love and were married in 1939 in Kano. Their son, Dan (known by the natives as Dan-Juma, which means Son of Friday), was born in December of 1940.

This dedicated couple then began pioneering an effective and difficult work amongst the Pagan people of Nigeria and they saw many Africans surrender their lives over to Jesus Christ. During their time in Nigeria, they faced many difficulties, including the burning down of their home, and Alf's many tropical illnesses that eventually forced them to make a dangerous sea journey back to war-torn England that almost cost them their lives as the German U-boats attacked and sank several of the ships in their Royal Navy convoy.

In this book you will read about how Alf was able to claw his way back to health and return to Nigeria, where he faced even more problems from the tropics, and eventually returned to Liverpool close to death. After recovering at the local hospital for tropical diseases, he was told that he must never return to the tropics.

But Alf and Anne Wooding never gave up and, despite this crushing blow, they eventually moved to the industrial city of Birmingham and started a work among the Jewish population of the city. Most of the Jews at that time had fled the Holocaust and were trying to pick up the pieces of their lives so devastated by Adolf Hitler's "Final Solution."

They also ran a little church called the Sparkbrook Mission and saw many of their "flock" become involved in missions—including two couples going to Nigeria to take their place there.

Anne and Alf Wooding were always deeply conscious that they were following in the footsteps of other great British missionaries like David Livingstone, Hudson Taylor and Gladys Aylward. Like them, "The Great Commission" of Jesus Christ to "preach the Gospel to every creature" was not an optional extra in the life of a Christian, it was the most important command that He gave us before he ascended to be with The Father in heaven.

The message of Blind Faith is that all of us, whatever our background, can follow Jesus to the ends of the earth with the message that can transform even the most intransigent sinner. For only He can take that Blind Faith and make it work in a way that none of us can ever imagine.

The question is: Are you willing to follow in Anne Wooding's footsteps?

Chuck Smith, Senior Pastor
Calvary Chapel of Costa Mesa
California, USA

TABLE OF CONTENTS

Chapter One

A DEATH IN
"THE CITY OF SHIPS"

Wearing a Church of England black and white nun's habit, Miss Underdown knelt by the bedside of Edith Blake, nee Tanswell, my 36-year-old mother, and pleaded with God to spare her life. A deaconess from St. Jude's Church, Kensington, Liverpool, England, Miss Underdown had been a regular visitor to our home in St. Jude's Place, and she now was only too aware that my mother was gradually getting weaker and weaker.

As I watched this middle-aged woman deep in prayer, a trickle of fear came over me as I noticed that my mother's red-flushed face had suddenly gone a deathly white, and I knew, even at the tender age of four, what was going on. My mother was reaching the end of her short life.

The year was 1912 and we were living in a terraced house in the port city of Liverpool, the "city of ships." It was a bustling place that had hosted some of the grandest ocean

1

liners like the *Lusitania*, which was later sunk at sea by the Germans, and the *Mauritania*. These "floating cities" would sail into the murky waters of the River Mersey from exotic places like Lagos, New York, Shanghai and Sydney, and then tie up at the landing stage, a floating structure, some 1,148 feet long. Hinged bridges connected the landing stage with the river wall. The western side of the river was lined with docks of the busy port of Birkenhead, in Cheshire. The great writer, Charles Dickens, had sailed from Liverpool to the United States on the *Britannia*.

Liverpool's commercial importance began to emerge in the 17th Century. In the 18th century the power loom began to make Lancashire the world's greatest cotton-manufacturing center and Liverpool, its chief port.

The city was a mass of contradictions — of riches and poverty, of massive Victorian commercial architecture and huddles of slum streets; of people who were as tough as the environment, yet could be extremely gentle and poetic.

Around the area where the Blake family lived, there were many Chinese wash houses, run by immigrants that had settled in the city after long sea journeys from China.

It would be many years before four young men from Liverpool, the Beatles, would take the music world by storm by singing, "All You Need Is Love." Love was something that we, as a family, had experienced from our parents, during the most difficult of times.

The foundation stone of Liverpool's Anglican Cathedral was laid by Edward VII in 1904, just four years before I was born on January 25, 1908. My mother had given birth to me in the very bed where she was fighting for her life. I was Christened as Anne, but soon became known as Nancy by all my family. I later discovered that my maternal grandmother's name was also Anne, and she had been given the nickname of Nancy, so it was decided to do the same with me.

Even as this dear Christian lady continued praying, my mother's eyes fluttered momentarily and she drew her last breath. The struggle was over!

"I'm afraid she's gone to heaven," said Miss Underdown in a voice barely audible as she rose from her knees and put her arms around me. "Your mother is now safely with the Lord."

I bit back on my lips, trying to take in what she had just told me, and then began to shudder with grief. I had hardly gotten to know my mother, and now she was gone, leaving Samuel Blake, my father, a former naval seaman who had traversed the oceans of the world in the days of sailing ships, to try to raise us children on his own.

"Ashes to Ashes"

My mother died on May 15, 1912, and her funeral took place five days later at West Derby Cemetery in Liverpool.

I watched sadly as Canon Bridge, the officiating minister, intoned the words, "Ashes to ashes, dust to dust," and then the coffin, bearing my mother's body, was lowered slowly into the freshly dug grave. My father picked up some soil and tossed it on top of the oak box.

My brother Eddy had missed the funeral. He had been in the hospital where he was being treated for his weakened legs caused by rickets, and so had not been aware of the tragedy that had occurred. Intensive therapy at Liverpool's Children's Hospital had helped him to walk properly and so, when he returned home, he wanted to proudly show his mother that he was now "normal" and to see that his steps were no longer faltering. He loved her very much and so, after arriving home, Eddy rushed into the living room and shouted, "Where is my Mummy? She has not been to see me for a long time."

My father looked at Eddy with deep sorrow in his eyes and was unable at that moment to respond. How could he explain to his son that his mother had been suffering from pneumonia and that she was now dead.

"Eddy, come and sit on my knee," my father finally was able to say, as he began to gather his composure.

My older brother ran to his father and hopped onto his knee. "Son, you mother's asleep," he said in a trembling voice.

Before my father could say anymore, Eddy jumped to the floor and ran up the stairs, taking two steps at a time, and dashed into his mother's bedroom. After not finding her, in sheer panic, he went to other rooms, but she was nowhere to be found and he came downstairs and yelled, "My Mum is not in this house. Where is she?"

My father, a rugged man with a large beard, decided he needed to try to explain to Eddy the real situation. "Your Mummy has gone to heaven," he stammered, "and if you are a good boy and love the Good Shepherd, one day you will meet her in the place where Jesus is."

Eddy began to cry. Huge tears fell down his cheeks and I joined in. I could not take so much pain. My elder sister, Ethel, also began to bawl in anguish. Alfred, my other brother, stood silently by, trying to be brave, his lower lip trembling.

Suffering—A Way of Life

Suffering was a way of life in the Blake family. We had already lost two sisters, Elsie and Edith, who had died as babies. Our three brothers, Charles, Samuel and Robert, had also passed away. Charles died, choking on a bone; Samuel fell down the cellar stairs and died of meningitis, and Robert died as a baby.

I comforted myself that they, at least, could gather around their mother in heaven.

Life in Liverpool at that time in the early years of the Twentieth Century, was extremely hard for people from the poorer homes. Our family was certainly not alone in seeing many deaths in the family. Medical treatment was expensive. There were so many illnesses that, today, would be easy to treat, like diphtheria and tuberculosis, but in those days, even with the proper treatment, could prove fatal.

I was puzzled by all of this death and I wished I could also go and join them in their heavenly home. It surely must be better, I pondered, than the hunger and pain of life in Liverpool at this time. I did not realize then that we were all traveling on a journey from earth to heaven as Christian in John Bunyan's *Pilgrim's Progress*, a book my mother had read to me. I had heard how Pilgrim had been fleeing from the wrath to come. He had to start at the cross and, even as a mite, I had realized that we all, too, had to do the same if we were to reach the eternal bliss.

Shortly after this, my father asked us to gather around him and he began to sing:

I have a mother in the promised land,
I have a mother in the promised land,
When my Father calls me I must go;
To meet her in the promised land.

He then encouraged us to join in and we raised our voices in unison to sing:

I have a mother in the promised land,
I have a mother in the promised land,
When my Father calls me I must go;
To meet her in the promised land.

We've got two sisters in the promised land;
We've got two sisters in the promised land;
When my Father calls me I must go;
To meet her in the promised land.

We've got three brothers in the promised land,
We've got three brothers in the promised land,
When my Father calls me I must go;
To meet her in the promised land.

His light shining through me, to others each day,
By his constant companionship all the way,
To bring other souls out of darkness to light,
Through the blood of our Savior, we'll win the fight.

We'll sing unto Him in the mansions of rest.
His praises we'll sound o'er the earth we have left.
"Glory," we'll sing to the Lamb, once slain.
We'll sing to his praise, again and again.

I loved my father deeply and I would sit on his lap as he would recount stories about his life of adventure in the Royal Navy as he sailed in the wooden sailing ships that would depart from Liverpool for long, and dangerous journeys, around the world. His red, callused hands gesturing as he spoke. I discovered that he had run away to sea from his home in Atherstone, a coal-mining town in Warwickshire, close to the Leicestershire border, and had been given much of his schooling on board the ship. He traversed the world several times. In those days, it would take three years to circumnavigate the globe.

My father's eyes would sparkle, as he recalled for me these tales of "battling the high seas" and the "strange people" found in foreign lands. Even as he spoke, I could tell that he was not well. My mother's death had taken a terrible toll on his health and he was often in agony from a trapped nerve over his eye after a fall from the rigging and so, after retiring from the Navy, he found himself unable to work.

Home of "The Blues"

Since he was unable to continue his civilian work on a minesweeper on the Mersey, we had to vacate our lovely home to move to a small, terraced house at 21 Boyd Street in hilly Everton. The house was located a short way from the famous Goodison Park, home of Everton Football Club — "The Blues".

I was now aged 5 and my sister, Ethel, was 14. One day Ethel took me and my brother Alfred, to see Aunt Lottie — my mother's sister — who, along with her husband, Ted, ran a public house (bar) in nearby Great Homer Street, Everton. We enjoyed seeing Lottie, who always warmly welcomed her only sister's children.

However, I did not realize that, at the time, she secretly blamed my father for my mother's early death. My parents had run a pub called Kaine's Hotel in Park Lane, Toxteth, and worked long, back-breaking hours, opening at 6:00 AM, and closing near midnight. My mother cooked for the dockers and this, along with the appalling burden of losing so many of her children, had placed an intolerable encumbrance on her. This family disagreement had caused Lottie and my father to drift apart.

After a few hours in her home, my aunt took Ethel to one side and said, "I think I could ease your father's burden by looking after Nancy until she is a little older."

When Ethel told me the news, I burst into tears and said that she could not "go home without me."

"You know that Daddy will be very angry as he loves me very much," I said.

Overhearing what I had said, Aunt Lottie reassured Ethel that "everything would be all right." She went on to add, "At your age, it will be difficult to take care of your younger sister. I know your Daddy will understand!"

With that, Ethel left and "rehearsed" how she would explain to our father what had happened. I prepared myself for a new chapter in my already eventful life with Aunt Lottie and her four-year-old daughter, Edith. We soon became firm friends and got on well together as I did with Norman, who was just 3.

* * * * *

Christmas Time

It was Christmas Eve of 1913, one year before the outbreak of World War I. King Edward VII was on the throne at the time and little did we know that soon he would be rallying our troops in Europe as we took on "Kaiser Bill" of Germany.

Edith, Lottie's daughter, and I had hung up our stockings by the roaring fire in anticipation that Santa Claus would come during that magical night and fill them with presents. On Christmas morning, we rushed down from our bedrooms, to find that some of the gifts would not fit into the stockings. The best gift for us girls were two prams (baby carriages) which already had dolls sitting pretty inside them.

Aunt Lottie had employed Ninny (a nurse) who wore a shawl, black bonnet and a smart long dress, with a high neckline with a white frill, to take care of us children. Ninny, whom I guessed was about 70 years of age, had a lifetime of service with children.

We girls were allowed to proudly push our new prams out onto the frozen streets close to our home. We got as far as the local park, to find it full of other children playing with their new presents.

As the cold winter months began to merge into the cooler Spring and then warm Summer, young Norman, Edith's brother, would want to join us on our expeditions. Fights would often break out between him and myself or Edith as he wanted to push our prams. An exasperated Ninny would have to jump into the middle of each fracas and try to stop our little fists from pummeling each other.

*   *   *   *   *

My heart began to pound with excitement when Aunt Lottie told me one day that my father was coming to see me. However, I was disappointed when he announced that I had to stay with my aunt "for the time being." To try to pacify me, he reached into his pocket and pulled out a watch and handed it to me.

"Keep this, and it will remind you of me," he said. "I will try and bring you home as soon as I can," he added.

I held it close to me and smiled tentatively.

Chapter Two

TIME FOR SCHOOL

Aunt Lottie's face was flushed with pride as she ad dressed Edith and myself. "I have been to see Miss Finley, the head teacher of the local church school in Great Homer Street, and we have agreed that you can both start there on Monday," she announced. "You are both five and I think it is time for you to begin your education."

Lottie was a deeply religious person and she had made the decision that it would be better for us to learn the "Three R's"— reading, 'riting and 'rithmatic' — at an Anglican school, where we would also get the basics of Christianity, rather than a state school.

Lottie had explained to us that the "C of E," as she called it, had separated from the Roman Catholic Church in 1534, and now had churches around the world within it called the Anglican Communion.

I did not know very much about school as I had not spent any time with older children. Besides being with Edith and Norman, I was usually playing with the sick boy across road and his illness had prevented him from attending an educational institution.

Ninny briefed us on what life in the classroom would be like for us and I began to look forward to this new stage of my life. "Children," she said as we sat on the floor before her on the weekend before classes began, "you will probably be given beads by your teacher to count and chalk to write on a slate."

Monday morning finally came and, after eating my breakfast of porridge and putting on my best dress, I joined Edith at the front door and Ninny headed out into the early-morning sunlight with her two charges on either side of her, tightly clasping her hands.

The Victorian Structure

All went well until we reached the Christ Church School building and, when I saw this huge brick-built Victorian structure rising up before us, and hundreds of children milling about in the play area, I began to have second thoughts about going inside.

"Couldn't I just come home with you and play?" I asked as my face puckered.

"No, Nancy, you have to go to school," she said firmly. "I know you will enjoy it.

So I reluctantly agreed to leave her with Edith at my side for whatever lay ahead for us. Both of us fought back the tears as we entered Miss Holmes' classroom, with its high ceiling. I noticed that many of the other children were already crying, so that reassured me that at least we were all in the same boat.

The kindly teacher stood before us, her brown hair in a bun and wearing a white blouse and long, black skirt, and welcomed us to her class. "Children, I know this is a difficult time for you, but let me tell you that a good education is vital if you want to get on in this world," she enthused.

"How many of you *don't* want to get on?" she then asked.

Miss Holmes allowed her hazel eyes to sweep around the room and seemed pleased when no one raised their hand.

"Good," she went on. "Now we can begin."

We were then asked to gather, along with the other pupils, in the large assembly hall and there the principal asked us to sing a hymn. She then asked us to bow our heads as she said a prayer for us all. After this, we were asked to repeat the Lord's Prayer, which we did in unison.

"The assembly is over and you can all go back to your classrooms," said Miss Finley as the air was filled with the scuffing of marching feet on the wooden floor as we all headed out for our lessons.

Each of the 60 students in our class, were given a slate and chalk and very soon the screeching of chalk was heard as we each began scribbling all kinds of things on the slate.

Hero Pig

After a few minutes, Miss Holmes called for "quiet" and then opened a book and began reading to us a story called, "The Three Little Pigs." As the story unfolded, I began to realize that the first two pigs were extremely foolish, but the third was clever and became a "hero pig" in my eyes.

I sat engrossed all through the reading. We had hardly been in the classroom for what seemed, to me, to be minutes, when Miss Holmes announced that we could now take a break and go outside to the playground for 15 minutes.

Edith and I quickly made friends with some of the other children and began playing "tag" with them and then eating our cookies that Aunt Lottie had thoughtfully supplied us with.

When the bell rang, summoning us back into school, I lined up with the others and marched back into the classroom. There, on our desks, we found a box of beads and a piece of white cotton with a needle. We were told to thread the cotton through the eye of the needle and then try to put the needle through each bead. After we had all been able to complete this task, Miss Holmes asked us to then follow her in counting up to ten.

Time flew by and, at midday, the clanging of a bell in the corridor outside told us that our classes were over for the morning. We headed for the cloakroom to gather up our coats and hats and we scurried along the sidewalk, for the half mile to our home to excitedly tell Aunt Lottie and Ninny all about our first morning in school.

Ninny had to hold up a hand to interrupt our flow of words because she could see that we would not have time to eat our lunch, before heading back to school. Ninny walked us back to the school and waited at the gates and waved to us as we went inside this time in a much more positive frame of mind. In fact, we almost swaggered into the classroom, confident that we were up to anything the teacher could throw at us during the next lesson.

"Good afternoon children," said Miss Holmes brightly.

"Good afternoon teacher," we responded loudly.

"All right," she continued, obviously satisfied with what she had heard, "I am going to ask you to write down a capital 'A,'" she said. Then said "A" in a powerful voice. "I also," she continued, "want you to write on your slate a small 'a' as well."

The teacher paused as we all vainly tried to write both down with our chalk. She walked around the class and nodded her head when she saw it was written correctly and murmured, "No, no" when she saw that a child had made a mistake. She finally returned to the front and wrote the correct ways on the large blackboard in front of her.

Days began to coalesce into months and both Edith and I loved our every moment at school. Our teacher had a knack of never making any of her charges look stupid in front of the others and appeared to possess the patience of Job in the Bible..

We loved to sing the mainly Christian songs that we were taught in "Assembly" and we made many friends in the schoolyard during the break time. I soon discovered that not all children were honest. They would cheat at games, though most played fair.

We were soon leaning to read and repeat the alphabet and count to 100.

A Step Further

The time came for all of us to progress to Class 2 and we children bade a tearful farewell to Miss Holmes. Our new teacher was Miss Jones, who was a little younger, than our previous schoolmistress but was equally as good. We now had to work harder as we were expected to copy down stories from the text books we were given and we also had to write down figures like 1,2 and 3.

As the Church of England is the state religion, we were given many lessons from the Bible. I particularly enjoyed hearing stories about Jesus loving the children and healing the sick and doing so much good during his time on earth.

"Do you know that Jesus, the Son of God, actually loved all of us so much that He allowed himself to be crucified on a cross at Calvary so that we could have salvation through believing in Him and what He did," she told us one day.

As I heard this, I felt great sorrow that Jesus had gone through such pain and agony for me personally. This was a love that I found hard to comprehend.

By now, my two brothers, Alfred and Eddy, had joined the school and I would meet them in the yard during breaks. One day, Eddy stopped me and said, "Nancy, I wish you could come home with us. We would be so glad to have you back as part of the family."

I felt a tear spill down my cheek as he said this. I began to realize how much I had drifted apart from them and my father. Because of his health problems, Eddy had only just started school and so had a lot of catching up to do.

"Daddy has been teaching me at home," Eddy proudly explained. "I am finding the lessons hard, Nancy, but I know I will soon catch up with the others." His prediction was proved correct, and he moved quickly up from class to class.

* * * * *

A long-standing tradition in Britain is the Harvest Festival, when people celebrate the safe gathering in of the summer harvest. We were all asked to bring fruit and vegetables to school and then, after gathering in the schoolyard, we all marched to the nearby Christ Church for a thanksgiving service. We were each asked to bring our gifts to the front of the church, the pillars of which were beautifully decorated with sheaves of wheat and corn.

The vicar, Canon Howell, then led us in singing the hymn, "*We plough the fields....*", and also "*All things bright and beautiful, all creatures great and small.*" After the singing, the vicar gave a sermon about the wheat and the tares growing together.

"This is symbolic for all of us here this morning," he began, his sonorous voice echoing around the packed sanctuary. "Each one of us will have our tares burnt up. When Jesus returns to this earth, He will gather us into His garner if we accept him as our personal Savior."

His words made me afraid in case my life was "full of tares" and I might be "burned up" when He came back to earth. But what should I do?

Chapter Three

BLIND FAITH

I was awoken by Ninny, who violently shook me and said, "Hurry up, Nancy. I have some news for you. Your Daddy is downstairs and you are going home with him."

I rubbed my eyes sleepily and thought I was hearing things. Surely this was not true. I dressed in record time and ran downstairs to find my father was, indeed, waiting for me. I ran into his open arms and he lifted me up and allowed me to kiss him on his bewhiskered cheek.

"Is it true Daddy?" I asked. "Am I really going home with you?"

"It is true!" he answered, his eyes twinkling with happiness. "We'll get your things packed up and then you are coming with me."

My uncle and aunt, along with Edith, Norman and Ninny, stood quietly watching the scene. Once I was ready to leave, I thanked all of them for being so kind. "I will never forget what you did for me," I told them.

I kissed each and then, tightly clasping my father's firm hand, I left to begin a new chapter of my life. I skipped along the cobble streets, the widest possible smile on my face, as we made our way past the rows of terraced houses, so familiar to the Liverpool street scene of that day.

* * * * *

Finally Reunited

My two brothers and one sister were older than I was. I was 7, and Eddy was fourteen months my senior, while Alfred was three years older than me. Ethel, was nine years older.

The threesome were waiting for me on the doorstep of our home in Boyd Street and the rest of the day was spent catching up with all our news. It was not long before I felt I was part of the family again.

Sundays were spent at St. Jude's, an Anglican church. We would all attend the three services, walking the one mile each way for the 10:30 AM, 3:00 PM and 6:30 PM services. If it rained too heavily, we stayed at home and took turns reading from the huge Family Bible that was prominently displayed in the living room. This Holy writ contained many lovely pictures of Biblical scenes that helped us to understand the King James version text. In the center of it was contained our family history with births and deaths included.

Daddy would never let us play out on Sunday. "This is a different day to all of the others," he explained. "It is the day we remember Jesus. That's why we call it the Lord's Day."

Over the next few years he would lead us in the singing of hymns. We had learned many of these songs during a week-long evangelistic campaign at our church school. I had sat transfixed as the speaker had talked about how we each had a "black heart" and then he explained how, "through faith in Jesus," our hearts could be washed white through the blood that had been shed on the cross by the Savior. He went on to say, "Don't forget children that red on black makes white."

Each of us Blake kids attended every meeting and I never forgot what the preacher had said. I knew that, with real paint, if you mixed these colors, you would get a muddy coloration and not white. But the man had explained that "black was our sin," and red was the blood that Jesus shed on the cross of Calvary for our sins. I realized that what he was telling us was that we had to accept Him into our hearts, confess our sin, and we were then made clean.

I was 10 years old now and on the last evening of the campaign, I made the decision to dedicate my life to God's service. I knew at that moment that one day I would be a missionary, but where and when I did not know!

* * * * *

I had, by now, reached the age of 14 and it was time for me to get a job. I had reached the top standard at Christ Church School and, like so many of my age, realized that I had to bring some money into the household. So I began to search for work. I also decided that I would continue my education at the local night school, so I knew I would have to get a job that would allow me time off to see to Daddy's needs during the day, while my brothers and sister were at work. It seemed a tall order, but I was willing to give it a try.

My father was still unable to work for much of the time because of his debilitating eye problem. I would wince as I would hear him cry out as the pain became unbearable.

One day I was reading through the classified ads in the *Liverpool Echo* when I spotted one for a job as a guide to a blind person. "The right applicant must know the district well, and must be able to work from 9.00 AM to 12.00 PM each day, and then from 2.00 PM to 4.00 PM," the advertisement stated. This seemed perfect for me. It was the same as school hours and so I took my pen out and wrote a letter to the address stated and applied for the job.

It was not long before the postman delivered a letter asking me to come for an interview at the home of a Miss Sarah Powell, the blind lady concerned. When I arrived, I was met at the door by her father. He told me up front that there were 19 other applicants to help his blind daughter. Fortunately, we hit it off immediately and he then brought Miss Powell into the room.

"The job, Miss Blake," he explained, "involves the successful person in guiding my daughter door-to-door while she attempts to sell goods to them from her suitcase."

"What kind of things does she sell?" I inquired.

"Tea, coffee, cocoa and boot-polish," she interjected, a quiet smile passing over her face. "They are all things that people need for their daily lives."

Never one to beat about the bush, I then asked Mr. Powell what the wages would be.

"I like your directness, Nancy," Mr. Powell chuckled. "I can pay six shillings a week. How does that sound to you?"

It sounded very good, especially as my brothers were only getting 10 shillings a week for a whole week's work.

"Well, Nancy, if you agree to my terms, I would like you to start tomorrow morning at 9 o'clock," he said. "You seem to be just the person to help my daughter."

I was overcome with joy. Employment at this time was difficult to come by, and jobs that brought satisfaction were even harder to secure.

"Blind-Self-Aid"

I arrived on time the next day and picked up the heavy suitcase as Miss Powell took my other arm and we headed out into the streets. On the case was a prominent red painted sign with the letters B.S.A., which stood for "Blind-Self-Aid."

"I have many regulars," she told me as we arrived at our first home and I rapped on the brass knocker of the front door. "A Mrs. O'Halloran lives here. She always loves my tea."

Soon the entrance opened and there stood the woman, wearing a white apron.

"Come inside and have a spot of tea with me," said the cheery Irish occupant. "And who is this pretty picture with you, Miss Powell?"

I was introduced and so began my whirlwind life as the aid to a blind door-to-door salesperson. Each day we would call on the regulars and then we would also do some "cold calling" whereby Miss Powell would explain what she was selling and offer a "special deal" if they would purchase from her.

"My goods are much cheaper than those at the corner store," she would tell each person on the doorstep as I would open up the case to show the wares on sale. Miss Powell was a thorough professional in her work and had very few refusals. After all, who could refuse a blind lady with a dewy-eyed teenage girl at her side?

At midday, I would accompany Miss Powell to her home and then hurry to mine to prepare a meal for my father and myself.

"Tell me all about your adventure this morning?" Dad would ask as I busied myself in the kitchen. I would excitedly recount each call and then we would sit together and enjoy Shepherd's Pie, or something like that.

A highlight of the week would take place on Monday afternoon, when Miss Powell and I would go to the women's meeting at St. Savior's Church. We both enjoyed the fellowship, but Miss Powell would also see the meeting as a sales opportunity. She was a member of the church and well liked, so most of the attendees would buy something from her at the end of the gathering.

I enjoyed the singing most of all, especially, "Oh Come to the Merciful Savior who calls You, O come to the Lord who forgives and forgets." Miss Powell often played the piano for the meeting as she was a good pianist.

Miss Powell would also send me postcards in Braille asking me to meet her for outings with other blind people "across the water" in New Brighton. I managed to begin to decipher the basics of Braille so I could read these messages.

At that early age, I began to wonder if I could ever become a missionary and specialize in working with the unsighted. But then, I would see how sick my father was, and realized that, even if I could raise the money to go into missionary training, he needed me to take care of him. This trap that I seemed to be in was making me very depressed and this caused me to wonder if I was indeed a Christian.

If only I could be sure of God and His forgiveness in my life. At that precise moment, I thought that no one could know salvation until the last minute of their life. Then, if one happened to be good, one would go to heaven."

To add to my confusion, Miss Powell's father suddenly became sick and I lost my job. He died and she then had nobody to look after her and had to go into special accommodations for the Blind. The combination of his death and losing my job, made me extremely depressed and even caused me to consider ending it all.

I remember sitting in a local park one day with Sheila, an 18-year-old girl I had met there, and confiding in her how despondent I was.

"I feel the same," she said. "You know, Nancy, I feel so down that I want to jump in the Mersey and end it all. Let's do it together."

I was shocked with her suggestion. I had sort of thought about this, but still I knew I could never go through with it.

"I will see you tomorrow," I told her after a few minutes. "I need to get home to take care of my Daddy."

Sheila said nothing and I headed back through the park and to my home. A few days later, I was reading through the *Echo*, when I was startled to see the headline, **"LOCAL GIRL KILLS HERSELF IN THE MERSEY."**

I felt my hands begin to shake as I read the tragic story. Apparently, Sheila had been serious about her threat and, one night, had thrown herself into the freezing waters of the river under cover of darkness and drowned.

I looked around, fearful that my father would see me reading this story. He knew of my friendship with Sheila and may have even suspected about my depression and how it might lead to my ending my own life.

The more I began to search for truth, the more it seemed to evade me. I tried changing churches and began attending St. George's (Anglican) Church, which was nearer to my home.

The Reverend Ingles, once a month would use a shortened form of the prayer book service on Sunday morning for us children. By doing this, we got used to using the Anglican Prayer Book.

I knew, however, that I was doing all of this to try to cover up the terrible shock of my friend drowning herself and my own secret desires to do the same.

Confusion Reigns

My life was by now a confusing mixture of spiritual doubts and a burning desire to become an overseas missionary. The problem I faced was that I did not know the Savior that I wanted to represent. Still, I had particularly become interested in Japan and had started to get literature from an organization called the Society for the Proclamation of the Gospel in Foreign Parts.

I was so interested that at the age of 18, I applied to this mission for training. But when I took the forms to my father to sign, he told me that he could not do it. "Nancy, don't you realize how dangerous this could be for you," he stated. "Haven't you heard of the Boxer Rebellion in China and the way that Christians are being burned alive there."

I tried to explain that I wanted to go to Japan and he said that this would also be a dangerous place to go.

Of course I knew, but I was not afraid

Despite my father's dire warnings, I also became deeply interested in China, which had many religions and dated back thousands of years in history. Although he was against me going to China, he still kept me enthralled for hours with stories of his visits to this mysterious land when he was a sailor.

"Nancy, I know that China is dangerous," he pointed out one day. "You see, the first time I arrived in Shanghai, I stayed in an inn by the harbor there and next morning, when I awoke, I discovered that I had been robbed of all my money and possessions except for the clothes I had slept in," he said. "I think that China is definitely out for you."

With my father not too keen in me going to the Far East, I thought I would now turn my attention to Africa. I never told him that I was now studying everything I could get hold of about this amazing continent. I was intrigued to discover how huge and diverse the continent was. I had read about people in some parts running around naked and living in mud huts to the Moslems of North Africa and Northern Nigeria, wearing their long flowing robes and some wearing a turban on their heads. The pictures I saw of them in books at the library made them look like people from Bible days. They did not seem to have changed very much since those times.

My insatiable search for information, finally brought me to a book on Kano, the walled city of Nigeria. As I read about it, it reminded me of Jericho in the Bible with high walls all around it. Kano had sixteen entrances, the wall was steep and so high that no enemy could ever scale it to harm the inhabitants. To add to the city's protection were soldiers at each of the entrances to the city. No stranger could ever enter without permission from the Emir (leader.)

The more I read about Africa, the more I began to feel that this was the place I was being called to, but then nothing seemed to open up for me and, with my father being so ill, it seemed impossible that I would ever become a missionary. I had promised God when I was only 20 years old, that if He opened up the way for me, I would dedicate my life to missionary work.

I had by now completed my night school course in dress making and also commercial studies, and had passed the examinations with distinction. But it appeared to me that the whole time of studying had been a waste of time. There was no job in the horizon and definitely no way I could ever become a missionary.

I still had not, at this time, developed BLIND FAITH.

Chapter Four

QUESTIONS, DOUBTS AND ANSWERS

I will never forget my confirmation. My father had bought me a lovely white silk dress, gloves and a veil. The ceremony took place at St. Jude's Church and my brother Eddy was also confirmed at the same time.

Confirmation is a ceremony in the Church of England (Episcopalian), that is supposed to follow on from child baptism, when you "confirm" those vows that were made on your behalf, usually in front of the local Bishop.

At the end of the colorful ceremony, all of us who had been confirmed, were invited to a party in the church hall the following evening. The excitement continued on the Sunday morning, when, after our mile-long walk to the church, we were allowed to participate in our first communion. I closed my eyes as the priest said, "The body and blood of Jesus" and handed me the wafer to eat and then came the wine. Alfred and Ethel, who had been confirmed previously, joined Eddy and myself at the altar.

Before giving us the communion, the priest said that, when he blessed the bread and wine, they actually turned into the Body and Blood of Christ. I found this difficult to follow. I had watched the service many times as a spectator, but now, because I was taking part in it, it became something very solemn for me.

Nail of Doubt

As I continued to grow into womanhood, I became a typical young person, questioning everything, including Christianity. Doubts seemed to grow inside my mind as each day passed by. Could Jesus be God? How could God become a baby, and why? How could the Blessed Virgin bare the Son of God? It was all very puzzling for me.

I eventually switched churches to one closer to home. My questions about the Faith were not helped when I saw on several occasions, the vicar in an inebriated state. It got so bad that on one occasion the Bishop had to reprimand him. As a punishment, the priest was sent away to another church. To me a drunken minister was no example to his flock. Still, this was just another nail of doubt that was being hammered into my faith.

One Sunday morning, instead of going to church, I decided to go for a long walk to visit West Derby Cemetery, where my mother was buried. As I stood by my mother's grave, I began talking to her as if she could hear me.

"Mom, I really miss you," I told her as the biting east wind whistled through the gray tombstones. "I wish I could have known you better."

After this, I still felt as cold inside as her gravestone on that winter's day. Nothing seemed to make sense anymore. I was seeking hard after God but I could not find Him.

In the Dark

One day, I opened the Family Bible in our home and fluttered the pages until I found the book of Job. In it I read the words, *"If only I knew where I can find him."* I took comfort from the fact that eventually Job did find God and was able to say, *"I know that my redeemer liveth."* I could see that Job was sure of God and that God had blessed him despite of all that he had been through. God brought Job to victory, but I was still in the dark.

I pondered on the fact that I was a member of a church and yet still did not have an assurance of salvation. If only I could know that God had forgiven me and that heaven was a real place. I so much wanted to go there and meet my mother and brothers and sisters again. It was not now as easy to believe as when I was a little girl.

No wonder Jesus used a little child to illustrate His Word and had said, *"Unless you become as little children, ye shall in no wise enter the Kingdom of Heaven."* He had also said in John 14, verse 6, *"I go to prepare a place for you."*

Even though I knew these verses off by heart, I had still not found assurance that they applied to me. But I was heartened to read one day, *"If you seek for Me with all your heart, then you will find Me."*

All Change

I had always loved singing and was in the church choir. I had two friends who were also in the choir and were members of the church. Their names were Gladys Burgess and May Wheeler. They worked among the children in the Band of Hope, an organization which warned against the dangers of "strong drink" and also helped with the children's services.

One Thursday evening, the three of us went for a walk around the area. It was now summer and the weather was balmy. As we walked along, the sounds of hearty singing could be heard at an open-air meeting being held in the street. We stood on the edge of a crowd that had gathered around and we listened to young people giving their testimonies on how they had found a faith in Jesus Christ and had been "saved." I had never heard this expression before and it intrigued me. They spoke with such assurance about what God had done for them and I knew this was something that I did not possess.

One young man, whose face shone as he spoke, said, "All I can tell you is that once I was lost and now I have been 'found' by the Lord Jesus Christ, God's only Son." He certainly spoke with authority.

They then began singing again:

Saved by His Power Divine.
Saved through new life supplied;
Life now is sweet and my joy is complete,
For I am saved, saved, saved.

As they continued singing this again and again, I knew that I could not join in. I was only too aware that I was not saved, whatever that phrase meant. My friends did not appear to have the same doubts as I did and they joined in.

It was an extraordinary experience and all the feelings I had once had about becoming a missionary began to flood back. As I was standing there, one of the young people came up to me and handed me a tract. On it was the "plan of salvation" and also advertised a language class for intending missionaries that was being held at Donaldson Street Gospel Hall, which was a stone's throw from Anfield, Liverpool Football Club's famous soccer stadium.

As I was reading about this, Gladys turned to me and said, "Nancy, why don't you go. I know you've always wanted to be a missionary."

I nodded and allowed my troubled face to break into a wide smile. "Maybe I will; maybe I won't," I responded.

The following Tuesday evening I arrived at the location. The class was due to begin at 6:45 PM and I was there on time. Standing at the entrance of the red-brick hall were a group of youths who tried to be friendly and asked me to come inside with them.

"No, I'm not going anywhere until the teacher arrives," I said, giving them a withering look.

It was not long after this that Jim Birbeck, a local builder, arrived and took me inside. I was introduced to the other students that included Florrie and Tillie Kyle, Bill Williams and several others.

As Jim began, he explained that Albert Thomas, a former missionary in South America, usually led the class, but he could not make it that night. So, he said he would go over the previous week's Spanish lesson.

"But before we do that, let's sing some hymns in Spanish," he said.

After this, he opened his Bible and read Romans 8 in this romantic language. He then asked us to repeat Hebrew 1:1, in Spanish. I joined in reciting, *"Dios abiendo ablado"* that means *"God has spoken."* We discussed the verb "to speak" and soon the revision was over.

"All right, the class is over," announced Jim. "Let's close in prayer — in Spanish of course."

"Are You Saved?"

As I gathered up my notebook and put away my fountain pen, Jim came over to me and asked, "Nancy, are you saved?"

"I haven't been lost yet!" I replied sarcastically,

Jim looked at me in a strange way. I stood my ground. Surely, he understood that I belonged to the Church and was even confirmed.

But Jim did not give up that easily.

"Nancy," he pressed on, "you *have* to be saved to receive eternal life. All you need to do is to surrender your life to Jesus Christ and confess your sins and He will cleanse you of your sins and come into your life."

I stood eye-to-eye with him, but said nothing.

"It is His blood that was shed on the cross at Calvary that atones for your sins," Jim added,

By now my mind was in a whirl.

"Why don't you just accept Christ as your Savior," he asked. I had to say that he did not give in easily.

"Nancy," he pleaded, "for the last time, won't you kneel and accept the Lord Jesus Christ?"

It was the word "last" that did it for me.

I began to think, "What if this is my last chance?" I remembered that I once made a decision before, but now I was not sure if I meant it.

Without saying another word, I sank to my knees and, as others stood around me, I began to pray out loud, "Lord Jesus Christ, I confess my sins and I ask you to forgive me and wash me clean through your blood and come into my life."

Life Eternal

Even as I stood to my feet and people began hugging me, I knew immediately that Jesus Christ was the Son of God. I had a deep assurance of my salvation. I had no more doubts about anything anymore. The joy in my heart at that moment made we want to jump over the moon. Now I knew the real meaning of the crucifixion. My sins were nailed to the cross. I was confident of eternal life with Christ forever. I knew Him, whom to know is Life Eternal.

The words from the scriptures, "*To as many as received Him to them gave He the power to become the Sons of God .... which were born not of the will of the flesh but of God,*" became all to real to me on that life-changing evening. I was experiencing a wonderful new peace in my soul.

After this had taken place, Jim guided me into the main meeting hall where a service was taking place. As I walked into the room, a crowd was singing, "*Oh Jesus, I have promised to follow Thee.....*" This was the hymn that had been sung at my confirmation, but now it had a new meaning to me.

They then began to sing, "*Rock of Ages, Cleft for me,*" and "Jesus Lover of my soul." These inspired words all began to fit into place for me. At last, all of my doubts had disappeared.

When the singing had concluded, Jim Birbeck went to the podium and said that they had a new "sister" and he then invited me to stand up and give my testimony to the packed congregation.

It was all smiles as I said, "Mr. Birbeck says that I am saved, but all I know is that I have accepted the Lord Jesus Christ as my Savior and something wonderful has happened to me.

There were shouts of "hallelujah" and "Praise the Lord," and I sat down as people reached over to shake my hand. I had never seen people act like that, but I felt the overwhelming presence of God. One by one, people stood up and prayed for God to keep me and bless me.

As I walked home that night, I felt I was walking on air. I felt so happy. At last I had found God and knew that God was real. I pledged to myself that I would tell everyone about Jesus. Now I could be a real missionary with a real message that Jesus is alive and was living in my heart. They may not believe me, but I would tell them just the same.

I wanted the whole wide world to know, but would they listen?

Chapter Five

THE WITNESS

On the following day, I met my friends in the street near our home and they were eager to learn how my language class had gone.

"I got saved after it," I told them, my eyes sparkling. "I feel that up until now, my life has had a missing piece, but now it is complete. It was like a jigsaw puzzle and I could not fit the final piece into place, but now the picture is completed."

May, the elder of the two, looked peculiarly at me. "What do you mean by 'You've been saved?'"

Her question prompted words to come tumbling out of my mouth as I "talked" her through my time of doubt and how I had been challenged by Jim Birbeck to give my life to Christ.

"It is very simple," I went on. "Jesus paid the debt for our sins to His Father on the cross of Calvary and, through His shed blood, we can be washed clean by repenting of our sins and accepting His offer of salvation."

The girls looked dumbstruck.

"Would it work for me, Nancy?" May asked, a quizzical look in her eye.

"Of course it would," I responded. "Why don't you accept Jesus right now?"

May paused briefly, glanced at her friend who appeared to be totally bemused with what was going on and then said, "All right, Nancy, I'd like to do it."

Saved on the Street

I asked May to bow her head and pray to the Lord for forgiveness and then invite Jesus into her heart. There, in the street, with children playing happily around her, she closed her eyes and began to pray and was "saved."

Gladys, however, was not impressed. "Come on girls," she said, trying to get us off this "religion kick."

She pressed on, "Let's go to the matinee at the local cinema. You promised to go with me last week."

I said nothing, but began walking toward my home with the girls in tow. When we arrived at the front door I told Gladys that I did not have any desire to go to the movies anymore. "Films are a fantasy world and I only want reality in my life now," I said.

Gladys was shocked, knowing how much I had enjoyed the celluloid adventures from Hollywood that would transport us to a glamorous world that was totally different from the stark reality of life in Liverpool.

"I'll pay for you if you can't afford it, Nancy," she offered, believing that I was making an excuse because I was broke.

"No, Gladys, I'm sorry, but I think I'll go inside instead and study my Bible," I said as I inserted my front-door key into the lock and opened the door.

Gladys stamped her foot petulantly and hissed, "This is the last straw, Nancy Blake. I'll never speak to you again."

With that, she grabbed May's hand and dragged her off to the cinema. May looked back in desperation at me, but said nothing, not wanting to further offend her friend.

A few days later, I met privately with May who assured me that she was still "going on with the Lord," but added that her friend was "incensed with both of us." We decided, there and then, on the street, to pray for Gladys.

"Mad and Stupid"

But still, the anger of Gladys continued unabated. One day, as we were together, Gladys stormed over to us and shouted, "You are both mad and stupid."

"How do you really feel?" I chuckled.

I had longed to be able to tell my father about what had happened to me, but I kept on putting it off. Finally, one day I came home from working as a domestic in a lovely home in Liverpool and, instead of going into the front room to give my father a kiss, I went upstairs and knelt down by my bed and asked God to give me something from the Bible to explain to him what had occurred.

As I leafed through the pages of my black leather Bible, I found Romans, 10:9, which said, *"That if thou shalt confess with thy mouth the Lord Jesus, thou shalt be saved."* As I read these words, I knew that now was the time to talk to my father.

I flicked through further pages and came to, Ephesians 2, *"You hath he quickened who were dead in trespasses and sins."* I then read the passage, *"By grace are ye saved ... the gift of God."*

As I examined these verses, I looked up towards heaven and said, "Thank you Lord for answering my prayers."

With that I raced down stairs to tell my father the news. As I entered the room he looked softly at me and said, "What have I done to my little girl? She didn't come in and kiss me before going upstairs."

I threw my arms around him and he sank into a soft green armchair and I started in. "Daddy," I said nervously, "I have something to tell you."

"Yes, I know. *It* happened to you on Tuesday night, didn't it?"

I was taken aback and said, "How did you know?"

"You have been a different girl since then."

"I hope you mean better," I said.

My father smiled and said, "Yes, better than I have seen you for a long time."

I paused for a moment, took a deep breath and then said, "Yes, Daddy, I was saved on Tuesday night."

He looked at me blankly, so I pressed on. I then read the whole of Ephesians chapter 2 to him. He listened without comment, but I did expect him to be angry because he did not like Mission Halls, and Donaldson Street Gospel Hall was just that.

However, he said, "My dear, I will give you one month of that life. Then you will be the same as ever."

I could understand his suspicions. My personality in recent times had been volatile and unpredictable to say the least, and so I know that he may have thought that this was just another of my rash decisions.

"Daddy, I hope it will last longer than that," I said. "It is so wonderful. You ought to accept Christ, yourself."

He shook his head. "Nancy, I have traveled the world and met many people," he stated. "They start a new thing, but it never lasts, and so I'll give you a month."

"We will see," was all I could say.

* * * * *

I would then begin to say "grace" at the table before my meals and, as I did, my brothers would joke with each other. "Our Nan is saved now," Alfred laughed one day. I decided not to respond, knowing they would soon get tired of their taunts and leave me alone.

Gladys Reappears

Three weeks after my conversion and two weeks after Easter, Gladys turned up at my new spiritual home, Donaldson Street Gospel Hall. May, who was now a regular attendee, had brought her reluctant friend with her to one of the services.

A fidgety Gladys sat next to me and, before the meeting began, she said, "Don't worry, Nancy Blake, I have no intention of getting saved, so don't look so happy."

I smiled at her and said nothing.

The music leader then introduced the first hymn and we all began singing it with gusto. I sneaked a glance at Gladys and noticed she had also joined in. When the "message" was preached by Mr. Huxley, one of the elders, Gladys kept her face as hard as stone, showing no emotion to what she was hearing. He then invited people who would like to accept Jesus Christ as their personal Savior to "come forward for prayer." I could see that Gladys was restive. Maybe God was dealing with her.

"We are going to sing a final hymn and those of you that the Holy Spirit has convicted, please come forward," he said.

The final hymn was,

Just as I am with one plea,
But that Thy Blood was shed for me.

I could not but help notice that Gladys had begun sobbing, huge, heartfelt sobs.

Even before the service had ended, Mrs. Rowland, one of the members, came over to Gladys and asked her if she would like to accompany her into the vestry. This was the very room where I had accepted Christ. She agreed and followed Mrs. Rowland into the room.

After the benediction had been pronounced, May and I sat in our seats praying silently for Gladys as she wrestled with the greatest decision of her life. Our prayers were soon interrupted when Gladys returned, her face radiant with joy.

"I've been saved!" she announced, as tears of joy rolled down her cheeks.

It did not take any arm-twisting for us to take part in the Thursday evening open-air meeting at the corner of Hamilton Road, close to the hall. This was the same meeting that I had first met up with these wonderful people.

"I would like to give my testimony," I told one of the leaders during one outreach. His face lit up like a lamp and told me to "go ahead."

So there, in front of a small crowd of onlookers, I began telling my story of how I had "wrestled with doubt" and then had been "saved by Jesus." The people listened respectfully, something that was unusual for my fellow Liverpudlians. Usually, there was at least one heckler who, in his catarrhal accent, did what he could to interrupt the flow of the speaker.

Then each Friday, our little trio would join others for a prayer meeting for the community. This was always well attended and all of us there would be greatly blessed and strengthened by the experience.

Saturdays were a time for us to go out socially. Often we would gather at the Pier Head to catch the ferry over to Birkenhead and then we would go on a ramble to the Wirral, or we would take our bicycles and ride around the beautiful lanes of this area. Besides the social fun, we would also take tracts with us and hand them out along the way and often we would take time out to hold an open-air meeting wherever we arrived. We called our outreach, "Two wheels for Jesus."

Chapter Six

A CAPITAL JOURNEY

My father sat in his chair in our home and closed his eyes, as he vainly tried to hold back the tears. "God," he prayed in a voice that cracked with emotion of the moment, "I come before you and ask you to take care of my daughter as she travels to London. Amen."

I stood up and went over to my dear Dad and flung my arms around him. "You have been a real blessing to me and I will do all I can not to let you down," I told him. "I'll write to you every week."

I had heard about Redcliffe Missionary Training College, which was located in Chiswick, West London. It was an all women's college that had a terrific reputation. After writing away for their materials, I had completed the application forms to become a student there — the first step to becoming an overseas missionary — and been accepted to start in September 1932.

After a succession of jobs, that time had now come!

When I arrived at Lime Street Station with its massive arched roof made up of thousands of panes of glass, on that

41

exciting morning in September 1932, I was surprised to see so many people waiting there to see me off to London. They included Albert Thomas from the Liverpool City Mission, Mrs. Elizabeth Swinburne and Mrs. Lamkin, two of my most faithful friends from Donaldson Street, in addition to other members of my Assembly.

"Well, Nancy, how does it feel to finally be heading off to London and college?" asked Mr. Thomas.

"Wonderful!" was all I could say. "I thought this day would never come."

The group gathered around me and began an impromptu prayer time for me and then, it was time to hand my ticket to a rail official at the barrier to my platform. He clipped a little hole in it and then I marched towards the train that was awaiting me. I was followed by the little group who had gotten platform tickets and were determined to give me a memorable send off.

I felt tears well up in my eyes as they again gathered around me on the platform before I boarded the express train to the capital. They sang several hymns and, as I climbed the steps to the train with my suitcase in my hand, I had real trouble controlling my emotions as I heard the familiar words of the hymn, "God be with you till we meet again."

Even as they were singing, a guard blew his whistle and waved his flag, and the locomotive began moving slowly away from the station, leaving me waving from a window as the train gathered speed and headed south. I prayed quietly, "Lord, I put everything in Your hands."

Fighting back the tears of joy, I found a seat by another girl from Liverpool, and began talking with her. I discovered that her name was Marjorie and she was also going into training, but at the Mount Hermon Missionary Training College in London. As the smoky terraced houses of Liverpool were exchanged for the patchwork green quilts of the Lancashire countryside, we exchanged our experiences of how we were converted and had been led to our respective missionary colleges.

In one corner of the compartment of the carriage where we were seated, was a woman who appeared to be nodding off and, in another seat, a clergyman wearing a "dog collar" was reading a book.

"Would you like some chocolate?" I asked Marjorie and she nodded and leaned forward and snapped off a piece of nut brown chocolate from the bar that my father had bought for me.

After a while, my bar was gone and so I accepted some of her chocolate and we talked and ate, the first part of the 200 or so mile journey to what was then the center of the British Empire.

For some reason, the cleric suddenly stood up and asked if he could sit between us. I was not sure if he was tired of hearing us constantly talk, or maybe he wanted to be part of the conversation. As he sat down and laid his book on his lap, I turned to him and asked, "Sir, do you know the Lord?"

He looked shocked at the directness of my question and, in a bid to deflect my inquiry, he explained that he was a Roman Catholic priest on his way back to Oxford, where he had a parish.

Which Convent Are You Going To?

"Which convent are you two young ladies going to?" he then asked.

"We are not Catholics," my friend said. "We're going to evangelical missionary training colleges in London."

His face carried a quizzical expression as he heard this response.

"I was listening to you both and you seem to have had marvelous experiences with God," he said. "I just took it for granted that you were going to be nuns."

The priest smiled and then added, "I have never met others that have had such experiences. You have convinced me that you are sincere in all that you say. You have more than I have."

I took that to mean that he had not yet had a personal encounter with Jesus Christ, so I opened up my handbag (purse) and brought out a couple of tracts with the titles of, "The Way of Salvation" and "Safety, Certainty and Enjoyment."

The priest, whom I guessed was in his early thirties, took them from me and promised to read them. "You know, girls, I don't think it is an accident that we have met in this way," he declared. "God must have led us to meet. He must be in it!"

When the train finally pulled into Snow Hill Station in Birmingham — the half way point for the journey — the priest stood up and shook hands with us both.

"I have to get off here and catch my connection to Oxford," he announced. "This has been the most interesting journey I have ever experienced. I hope that we can meet again sometime. Every blessing to you both!"

We waved good-bye to him at the window of the corridor as the train started off again. On re-entering the compartment, we were surprised to find the lady who was sitting there sobbing. I went over to her and put my arm around her.

Are you ill?" I asked.

She shook her head and valiantly tried to compose herself.

"No," she said, "I have known the Lord Jesus for many years, and yet I have never had the courage to tell anyone. As I listened to the two of you talking about your experiences and then to that priest, I felt terribly convicted to think that I have never told a soul about my faith."

"Well, you have told us, so that's a beginning," I said. "Now you can begin to tell others."

Her face cleared as she understood what I had said.

"Why don't we pray for you now — and also our new friend, the priest."

The three of us bowed our heads and soon the compartment was full of prayer and praises. We continued discussing our lives with Christ, and before we realized it, our train was pulling into Euston Station in North London and it was the time to disembark.

By now the woman's face was radiant, and she hugged us both and thanked us for helping her to gain courage to be a witness for Christ. We left our new-found friend in a much happier frame of mind than when we had first begun talking with her.

A Capital Life

It was also time to part from my other friend.

"Well, Nancy, I must leave you now," said Marjorie. "I'll be catching a taxi outside. Maybe we could write to each other."

With that we exchanged addresses and she, too, was off, and I was left alone to try to find the right bus that would take me to Chiswick, a lovely suburb close to the winding River Thames. I wished I had the time to be a tourist for a few hours and see Buckingham Palace, the Houses of Parliament and the Tower of London, but I knew this was not possible.

It took an hour for the red double-decker bus to amble its way from the Euston district to Chiswick and I got off at Grove Park Road, where the college was located. As I walked along carrying my suitcase, I began to feel apprehensive about what lay ahead. Would I get on all right? This was an entirely new life for me in an enormous city that made Liverpool seem like a village.

I was already aware that Redcliffe, a missionary training college for missionary trainees, was founded by a Mrs. Tothan at Redcliffe Gardens in Chelsea, in the previous century. Then the institution moved to Chiswick and, incidentally, is now based in Gloucester.

As I continued down Grove Park Road with its magnificent houses, I noticed a wall with jagged glass on the top. I guessed this must be the outside of the college.

I rang the bell on a doorway cut into the wall and the gardener directed me along the garden path to the front door of the college. As I walked along the pathway, I spied the River Thames close by with its water shining in the early evening sun. The garden was in full bloom and looked so lovely. I suddenly forgot all about my nervousness. I was enveloped with a sense of freedom and I knew everything would work out well.

As I entered the front door, I was warmly welcomed by the staff and students. I was shown to my room by Miss Ivy Naish, the Vice Principal. As she shut the door after me, I suddenly felt free in this lovely place.

* * * * *

The Gong Show

While deep in my thoughts in my room, the reverberation of the gong at the bottom of the stairs, made me jump. It was obviously summoning us to the evening meal. I had just finished washing my face and generally tidying myself up after my long journey when a woman in her early twenties opened the door and took my arm.

"Come along, Nancy," she said. "We must never be late at the table."

As we went down the stairs together, she introduced herself as Winnie Rainsbury.

"I'm your room mother for the term," she explained. "There will be three of us together and I'm the senior one of us."

The dining room was very pleasant with several tables, six people at each. I followed Winnie to a table by the bay window that gave a splendid view of the famous old river and the mass of color of the garden.

We stood for the "grace" when one of the staff members asked God's blessing on the food and then we sat down to a salad meal and a sweet (dessert).

When we had finished, Winnie introduced me to my other roommate, Vera. She was not as friendly as Winnie and I was not sure that she liked me very much. Soon Vera became extremely abrupt with me and appeared to enjoy handing out lectures, saying that I "must not" do this or that here, "or you will soon be on the carpet."

Vera appeared to have a grudge against everyone. Her negative attitude caused my nervousness to return again and I began to feel fearful. After seeing over the whole house with Winnie, we all gathered together in the staff room where those of us who were newcomers were welcomed. The old students welcomed the new with friendly handshakes. We were seven, the perfect number — Mary, Rosy, Muriel, Miriam, Grace, Edith and yours truly. Miss Naish then told us about the upcoming new term.

The two head girls, Nan Gibson and Ivy Roberts, were then asked to stand and we politely applauded them.

Miss Miall, who taught Old Testament studies, then gave us a "word" from Jeremiah in which said that each of us should be, "*Clay in the Potter's Hand.*"

She added, "You are all clay to be molded into His Way."

Miss Naish closed in prayer, committing us all into "His care" for the night. So ended the first night at Redcliffe.

Next morning I awoke with a start and wondered where I was, or was I dreaming? A terrible noise had wakened me. It was the gong at the bottom of the stairs telling us that it was time to get up. I blearily checked my watch. It was 6:00 AM.

Then Vera appeared in the room with a cup of tea and a biscuit (cookie.) She was on tea duty for a month with another student.

I washed and dressed and, with Winnie's help, turned my mattress. The gong went again,

"It's time for our hour of quiet time devotions," she explained.

We drew screens around our beds so that we would have privacy. I knelt by my bed for one hour in quiet meditation and prayer. Also, Winnie had given me a verse of scripture to be learned and recited at the table before breakfast. I enjoyed that hour. It was a great help and strength to me.

Then, once again, the silence was broken by the discordant sound of the gong, telling us that it was time to make our bed and tidy our part of the room. Then I was told by Winnie that I had to clean the landing, stairs and hall with the help of another student.

At 7:55 AM, the gong sounded again. That meant that we had to hurry and prepare for breakfast by 8:00 AM prompt. We stood around the table and each of us students repeated the verse of scripture learned. We sang the hymn, "*I need Thee every hour*," had a prayer from Miss Naish and then she again said "the grace."

We sat down to eat warm porridge (oatmeal) with milk and sugar. It was good, but the Kedgeree that followed was new to me. It was boiled rice, hard-boiled egg and boiled fish all mixed together. I soon became used to it, as we often had it for breakfast.

When it was over, we had to finish the job allotted to us — I had to clean the toilets, staircase and landing, and then back to the bedroom to make sure it was tidy and ready for inspection by the staff.

Miss Naish paid a visit to my room and reprimanded me.

"Nancy," she said, "your bedcover is slightly out of place."

Accept Everything

Her reproach seemed silly to me and I thought she was just picking on me. It made me feel angry. When Miss Naish had left the room, Winnie took me aside and gave me good advice. "You must learn to accept whatever happens, as you are here to train and detail is very important in God's work," she pointed out.

Her counsel helped me to accept many things that I did not understand during the term, and throughout my training. I soon learned to say, "Lord you brought me here, so please give me the grace to accept and the humility needed."

At 8:55 AM we were to be in the lecture room ready to listen to the lecturer at 9:00 AM The timetable had to be carefully studied to find out which lecture to prepare for and all books needed on the desk in readiness.

Our first lecture was on Comparative Religions and I found it difficult to keep up with the lecturer. I did not own a fountain pen like the others. Ruth Sibly, who sat next to me, handed me a pen and insisted on me keeping it as she had several. It was a very good writing instrument and I was grateful. Now I did not have to keep dipping it into the inkwell with the basic pen that I had been provided with. She also let me copy the words that I had missed. I was relieved that I was able to correct it before I submitted my notes to be corrected by the teacher.

Monday afternoon was the Missionary Prayer Meeting, when we scanned missionary magazines for items for prayer. Also, missionaries would come to speak to us from different societies. After that, we would pray for the different needs of each one of them. We would close with a missionary hymn. One of my favorites was *"Lord speak to me that I may speak...."*

I gradually began to become acquainted with each of the new students and their different habits become indelibly imprinted on my mind.

Fruit of the Spirit

All the bedrooms bore the names of the fruit of the Spirit, such as gentleness, goodness, faith, joy, peace, patience, etc. For my first term, mine was in "gentleness." Each term, we changed to another room.

We would all go to church on Sunday morning, but the rest of the "Lord's Day" was usually spent taking Sunday School classes and evening meetings at London churches

During my time, I loved to scribble down pieces of poetry that just came into my head. One poem I wrote went like this:

My prayer that God would open the way
if He had willed me to go,
To train for further service, for Him,
while here below.
I prayed the way might open up,
if He had willed me go,
To spread the news that
He had given His life for us below.
The Potter needs to mold the clay,
and frame it for His way,
That it might be of use to Him,
in His own planned way.

It summed up very well what lay ahead for me!

As my sixth term at Redcliffe was completed and the "breaking process" continued my life, I added the following:

But this was still to be continued
Till His will was my will.
I felt things were a burden,
More than one could bare.
He said, "Cast they burden on the Lord,
and He shall sustain thee."
I rather slowly did it,
But it brought victory.
For He carried and bore it,
Because it was my plea.
My training days were finished,
But He had just begun,
Breaking and melting accomplished,
His molding through His Son.
The Christ-life, it was seen without;
His beauty it must be;
If others helped by us about,
It must be Him they see.
His beauty is so perfect;
Ours so stained by sin;
He's the altogether lovely One,
He must shine within.
Lo the peace My Savior gives,
Peace I never knew before;
And my way has brighter grown,
Since I learned to trust Him more.
That it might be of use to Him,
in His own planned way.
We'll praise Him for all that was difficult,
We'll praise Him for breaking too:
For melting, molding, and filling:
And bringing His likeness through.

BLIND FAITH

Chapter Seven

THWARTED BY MUSSOLINI

One day, I received a letter from the London head quarters of SIM saying that I had been accepted for Ethiopia. The letter also advised me to "wait for a while" as Mussolini was in Ethiopia and was sending all Protestant missionaries home to their different countries.

What had occurred was that Benito Mussolini had longed to create a new Roman empire and to bring back Italy's lost gory. To this end he trained a large army and built up the Italian navy. In 1935 he attacked the weak, backward, and poorly defended African country of Ethiopia. It was conquered the following year.

"They say that the door has closed there for the time being, so I will just have to be patient," I told a friend.

I also shared with this friend about how the interview had gone. "They teased me and asked if I had ever killed anyone with a hypodermic needle," I said. "When I laughed, they decided that I had a good sense of humor and would be suitable."

Swiss Cottage

I began to realize that if I was to work in Africa, I would need some medical training, so I applied to St. Columbus Hospital at Swiss Cottage, which was located in the north of London. When I arrived at Waterloo Station in London, I found my way to the underground (subway) station. I took a "tube" train to Swiss Cottage. The hospital was opposite the station. It was a very busy road and I had to cross carefully. On my arrival — on June 1, 1936— I was welcomed by Matron Dallon, who welcomed me and introduced me to the staff.

She beamed as she said, "Miss Blake, we hope that you will be very happy among us."

It was a Christian hospital and scripture texts were painted on the walls of each ward. Each morning at 9:30 AM., those that were well enough, would gather in one of the wards for a service. Patients were allowed to choose their favorite hymns, then one of the staff would lead in prayer and give a testimony about what God meant to them. Many of the patients accepted the Savior through these meetings or, sometime, during their stay in this hospital, through the personal witness of a staff member.

So, after my wonderful time at Redcliffe, I was now working at this hospital. However, I did not get off to a good start and my first week was terrible. My job was to gather up the bedpans, dispose of their contents, and then clean them in the sluice. The smells were awful. I felt too sick to eat and began to feel ill and irritable. Everything got me down.

However, I had to finish the month out to fulfill my contract which was on a month to month basis. On noticing my glum expression, Sister Howlett took me on one side for a chat. She explained that she had been a missionary in India.

"Miss Blake you will have to face many more difficulties than dealing with bedpans if you plan to be a missionary in Africa," she said. "You must persevere, otherwise you will never make it on the mission field!"

She was right of course and, once my attitude became more positive, I was allowed to do dressings on the wounds of patients.

One day I wrote to Mrs. Backhouse, a lady I had worked for, telling her how I had felt. I received a letter back by return of post saying, that she too felt exactly the same when she first went to St. Columbus' but after the third week she began to become used to it. "Nancy, get interested in the different patients and nurses and stick it out," she advised.

By the end of the month I was really happy. I started a prayer meeting for the off-duty nurses and was surprised to discover that some of them were not "born-again" believers. I even had the joy of leading Nurse Stormont and Nurse Clarke to know the Savior. They started coming to the meetings on a regular basis and were rejoicing in their new-found faith, and proved to be a strength to each other.

Matron was very pleased with us and encouraged us to help the younger ones grow in the Christian Faith.

Soon I was assigned to the men's ward. There were three in all: the TB (tuberculosis) Ward, Cancer Ward and Paralysis. They were all very sick people and needed a great deal of patience and understanding.

Mr. Asbury, a TB case, had to have oxygen given to him every fifteen minutes. The patient next to him had meningitis. He was an "urgent note," meaning he was not expected to live more than a few hours. The other TB patients needed plenty of fresh air, so the windows were left open, and, of course, good, nourishing food, especially fruit. They were a grand lot and teased the nurses and made them laugh.

The smaller ward had cancer and paralysis patients. They were all very seriously ill people. Mr. Wells was a very trying man, but he had need to be, as he was helpless. He would constantly call us to turn the page of his book and he would erupt into explosive anger if one of the nurses passed by without coming to him. I began to notice that some would avoid him as he was so difficult to get on with.

I tried hard to help him all I could, but he was still ungrateful. I prayed much for his conversion. He was hard and ridiculed all religion.

Candles for Billy

Opposite him was Billy, who had lung cancer and this was his 21st birthday. His mother and family came to the ward to celebrate it. He was not expected to live long. It was all very sad. They brought gifts for everyone in the ward. There were candles on the cake for Billy to blow out. He always put the "best side" out when his mother came so they all had a happy afternoon. I took great interest in him. After helping Sister with his dressings on his terrible wounds, I realized all that he must be going through. I would go and have chats with him about the Lord Jesus Christ. I would put the screen around him so that he did not feel embarrassed. One day he accepted the Lord into his heart and his face was radiant.

Minutes later, Mr. Wells, who was in the bed opposite, called me to him and asked, "What has happened to Billy? His face is shining, yet he suffers so much. How can he be happy? I am being taught so much by him." I was able to explain to him about what conversion meant.

* * * * *

China Odyssey

The service began at a local Parish church and then a missionary from China, preached the sermon. I was extremely tired, having just come off night duty. All that I heard was "Is there someone here, already trained and sitting back, when the need on the field is so vast?"

However, I did nothing for a week about this challenge. I went back to the same church as the previous Sunday morning. I sat praying for a while and then made a decision. "I will apply to the SIM tomorrow Lord, to go to another field of service in Africa."

So on Monday morning, I rang the British SIM general secretary, Mr. Robert Horn, on the phone and asked, "Is there a need for a worker among the blind in Nigeria?"

"There certainly is," he replied. "Could you come here tomorrow for an interview with Dr. Roland Bingham (Director of SIM and a founder.) He has just arrived from Nigeria." I went to the interview and nervously awaited its outcome.

Mr. Horn then rang the Matron at the hospital asking for permission to see me. Naturally, she agreed to this request.

During our get-together in the nearby nursing home, he said, "Miss Blake, I want you to go to the Liverpool School for the Blind for a three month course, and learn the practical side of it, making baskets, trays, chair caning, mats, etc.

"Then, if all goes according to plan, I would like you to sail to Nigeria to teach the blind there."

At last it appeared that I would leave for Africa! But first I had to successfully complete the course in my home city!

Chapter Eight

A JOURNEY INTO SPACE

The sights and sounds of my beloved Liverpool soon became familiar again to me. The "Scouser" accent, a strange amalgam of English, Irish and Welsh, all mixed up together, was again a joy to hear. The city, a mass of contradictions — of riches and poverty; violence and humor, brutal Victorian commercial buildings, huddles of slum streets and neat suburbs where the middle-class lived.

One of the first places I went to see was the twin towers of the Royal Liver Building that rose majestically into the sky and the city's most familiar sight to the thousands of travelers who arrived in England by liner from New York and other major cities of the world.

I gazed out onto the murky waters of the River Mersey, and tried to imagine how I would feel when I eventually boarded my big ship bound for Lagos, Nigeria, for my new life as a missionary.

A New Home

A pleasant surprise for me was the fact that my family had moved to a beautiful semi-detached house in Oakhampton Road, located in the pleasant suburb of Childwall. The area was very middle-class and each home in the road had a lovely back garden with a lawn. It was completely different from the cramped quarters we had lived in in Everton, a decidedly working-class area of the city.

I was free for one month before starting at the blind school, as it was closed for the holidays. This gave me the opportunity to call on my relatives and friends, whom I had not seen for a long time.

I took the bus to Anfield and went to Donaldson Street Gospel Hall for the Sunday morning meeting. It was an emotional reunion with people like Mrs. Swinburne, Mrs. Lamkin, Florrie and Tillie Kyle, Mr. and Mrs. Huxley, Mr. and Mrs. Watson and Mr. and Mrs. Roberts as well as Jim Birbeck, who had been responsible for my conversion. My friends, Gladys Burgess and May Wheeler, were also there.

I had much to talk about and I was asked to bring everyone up to date about my plans. The month just flew by and my family hardly saw me.

It was soon time for me to start at the School for the Blind, in Hardman Street, in the downtown area of the city.

I was received by the three teachers, Mr. Stevens, Mrs. Williams and Miss Gones. They were the main teachers and they welcomed me to their midst.

As the class of 6 settled in, I was asked to tell the other students about the reason I was there.

"I have been selected to go to Nigeria in West Africa as a missionary to teach the blind people there to read and write in Braille" I explained.

On hearing this, gasps of pleasure echoed around the classroom.

"Miss Blake, and all of you gathered here this morning," said Mr. Stevens, "can be assured that we will do all we can to give you the knowledge you will need in your upcoming careers."

During the break, three of the girls there, Edna, Nancy and Laura, gathered around me in a cafeteria and peppered me with questions about why I was going to Africa, and I was able to share my testimony with them. Then I told them about the different peoples of this huge country, their customs and the geography of the land. I had read all of this up before I had started at the school. They never seemed to get tired of asking questions.

The Origins of Braille

Mr. Stevens then proceeded to give us a history lesson about how Braille was invented.

"Louis Braille, who was born near Paris, France, on January 4, 1809, accidentally blinded himself at the age of three," he explained. "When he was ten years old, he entered a school for the blind in Paris. At that time blind persons read by touching letters engraved in wood, cut in cardboard, or cast in lead."

Our instructor said that this was such a "cumbersome and slow" method for reading, that no blind person could write with such a system.

"Young Braille learned about a writing technique that had been invented by Charles Barbier, a French army officer," he continued with his fascinating lecture. "It was a 12-dot system that was punched on cardboard for nighttime battlefield communications.

"Braille devised a similar system using six dots in 1824. When he was 15 years old."

He then said that Braille, who had been teaching at the School for Blind Youth in 1826, published his system in 1829 and the students readily accepted it.

"Because it differed so from standard printing, other teachers were reluctant to use it. This delayed adoption of the system by the school until 1854, two years after Braille's death."

Mr. Stevens then stated that, within the next 20 years, other dot-reading systems were developed in the United States. These, along with Braille's system, were used in the United States until 1916, when Braille's original dot alphabet was adopted.

"The universal Braille code for the English-speaking world was adopted in 1932 at a conference in London," he went on. "This is known as Standard English Braille, grade 2. This is what we will be teaching you during your time here."

He then got to basics with us. "The Braille system consists of 63 dot patterns, or characters," Mr. Stevens said. "Each character represents a letter, combination of letters, common word, or grammatical sign. "The dots are arranged in cells of two vertical rows of three dots each." He then went on to explain the more intricate basics of the system.

Mr. Stevens had heard that I had learned the Braille some years earlier — when I was 14-years old — and so called me to the front to read the embossed letters of the Braille version of the *Reader's Digest* to the other students. They each had a copy and did their best to follow along with me, but I could see that it was early days for most of them, and some looked as if they were going to cry, wondering how they would ever master this strange new language.

Each morning, at 9:30 AM, we would assemble in the main hall of the institution for prayers. Then, we would go to the allotted work assigned to us. I was making a string stool. I also learned to cane chairs. I kept a note book to jot down material required, the amount that would be needed and during those periods, I made a pretty tray and a teapot stand to match it.

One Month to Go

I still had one month before sailing for Africa and each day was packed with activity. I would speak at three or four meetings a week at churches in the city where people there wanted to know about my plans. Gifts were given and people promised to pray for me and also correspond. All this gave me more confidence and courage, for I knew that only what the Lord did through me would count spiritually.

I had met three blind girls during my time at the school and I invited them to my home, because I wanted my father to become familiar with the kind of people I would be working with.

"Nancy, " I don't think this is a good idea," he had told me. "I know I will feel sorry for them and I won't know what to say."

"Don't worry, Daddy," I told him. "I think you will be in for a pleasant surprise."

I was right! My father was so astonished at their happiness. They soon had him laughing with them. So the evening ended and they went safely back home.

A farewell meeting at Donaldson Street Gospel Hall was scheduled on the night before I was due to sail to Africa. The assembly room was packed and there was tea and cakes provided for everyone after the service. Special invitations were sent to my family, and they sat at the front of the hall, while I sat on the platform. I had to speak about my call to the mission field and also tell about what kind of work I would be doing out there. It was a wonderful meeting. Once it was over, I knew that within hours I would be making the greatest trip of my life.

The Abosso

I was up early next morning, November 3, 1937, for this was the day I was to sail to Nigeria on the Elder Dempster

Ship, *The Abosso*. My father, sister and brother, accompanied me to the Pier Head, on a Number 4 tram. Then we walked to the nearby Princess Dock. My family had special passes to join me on board.

I could see from his wide smile, that my father was thrilled to be on board ship again even if it was only for a short time. I was busy seeing the purser and Miss Hignet, secretary from the Sudan Interior Mission Headquarters' in Liverpool. She had to give me final instructions for the "upcountry" journey when I arrived in the port of Lagos.

"It will take two days journey by train for you to arrive in Minna," she said. "You should get a purser on the ship to pack you enough food and drinking fluids for the trip."

Mrs. Williams from the blind school was also on the ship with Edna, Nancy and Laura enjoying themselves. Mrs. Williams introduced me to George, the Chief Steward. He was a friend of hers. He said that he would see that I was made comfortable for the whole journey. The three girls had a chat with me and promised to write to me, which they did.

Mrs. Swinburne, Mrs. Lamkin, Charlie Molloy and many other friends from Donaldson Street Gospel Hall were also on board to see me off. In all, some fifty people had gathered there.

I could see that the Purser was getting agitated with the crowd.

"I've nothing to do with it," I told him. "All I know is they all have tickets."

It was then that I realized that others, who were making the trip, had no one to see them off.

Then I heard the announcement over the PA system, "All visitors have to leave."

As I embraced each one of them, they left and the gangways were pulled up.

Lots of Waves

I leaned over the side of the ship and waved to all my friends. They started to sing me off "*Jesus Shall Reign, Where 'ere the Sun,*" and then "*God Be With You, 'til We Meet Again.*"

I noticed that the blind girls were still waving until the singing had died away and we began pulling away into the Irish Sea and then the Bay of Biscay.

Then at last I was able to relax. I had not been to my cabin yet as there had been so many people to say good-bye to. So, when I arrived there, I found it full of presents. I was so surprised. There were chrysanthemums, which the stewardess took away to put into a vase, then returned with them. They looked lovely. There was also chocolates, sweets (candies,) several books, including *Streams in the Desert*, from Mrs. Swinburne. She was my spiritual mother. It was all so exciting for me.

Miss Nancy Munro, my cabin mate, however, did not appear to be very pleased. She did not have anyone to see her off and was annoyed at all these visitors walking in and out of the cabin. She was from Glasgow and had been trained at the Bible Training Institute there, and was to be my companion all the way to Africa.

"Nancy," she said, "there was a really nice young man at BTI called Alf Wooding. He will soon be joining us in the language school at Minna. He might make a good 'catch' for one of us."

* * * * *

We were nearing the Bay of Biscay, the boat was beginning to rock as the sea is usually stormy there. I felt quite nauseous and the stewardess made me lie down on my bunk. She made me comfortable and then brought my evening meal to the cabin.

Miss Munro had to go alone to the dining room. Next morning I felt better as all the sickness had gone.

Margaret and Ann, two other new-found friends, made us laugh. They were leaning over the side of the ship, feeling so sick. I told them, "Now we understand why we had to make out a will before we got on board ship. We'll never survive this journey."

It was truly to be a journey into space!

Chapter Nine

LEARNING A NEW LIFE STYLE

I gazed out from the deck on the scene below on that eventful day for me — November 19, 1937. There were bronzed, sweating bodies buzzing around like worker bees, as they began unloading the ship at Lagos. I smiled with joy as, at last, I was in Africa. I had to admit that this was nothing like the Pier Head in Liverpool, which I had left some 16 days before. There were natives lined up begging for money and the weather was like a sauna.

I took out a handkerchief and wiped my brow, but within seconds the perspiration had returned. I soon discovered that Nigeria's climate is shaped by the moist, unstable air to the south and the dry, stable air of the Sahara to the north. We were now sweltering in the southern region where humidity and temperatures are high all year round.

I went back to my cabin and supervised the Nigerians who were there to help carry my suitcases and a trunk packed full of tropical clothing. One of the porters picked up the heavy trunk and lifted it up onto his head as if was as light as a feather. We were followed by Miss Munro's porters.

At the bottom of the steps from the ship, we were greeted by Mr. Merryweather, who along with his wife worked with the Yoruba tribe. She also was there to shake my hand.

"Welcome to Nigeria," said Mr. Merryweather, in a friendly fashion. "I hope the trip wasn't too rough. That Bay of Biscay can get pretty terrible at times."

We had to agree, but all of the seasickness we had experienced, was now a thing of the past. I was excited to finally be in the land that God had called me to.

The customs area was a scene of total chaos with passports to be shown, and luggage to be searched by Nigerian and British officials, who were there to try and bring a semblance of order to the situation. We were an hour, or so, in customs as we all had a lot of luggage with us.

Peace in the Storm

The Merryweathers' hovered around me and Miss Munro to make sure that we encountered no problems. My head began to spin, but they remained calm, and finally we were both waved through.

"It's time to catch the train," Mr. Merryweather said. "Just follow me and I'll get a taxi to take us to the station." Porters again picked up our items and followed us outside, and he slipped a tip to each of them.

He bartered with the driver before we got in an ancient black British car. Mr. Hummel, the leading missionary at the SIM Jos office, also ordered a taxi. I watched in awe out of the window at the extraordinary press of people in the streets of Lagos. I pointed out to Mrs. Merryweather, a woman carrying a baby on her back and a heavy pot on her head. I marveled that the baby did not get hurt.

"You'll soon get used to these scenes, ladies," she chuckled. "After all, this is Africa and you'll find just about everything different from home."

When we arrived at Iddo Station, the taxi driver asked for more money for the short journey. When Mr. Merryweather refused to pay the extra amount, the irate driver, got out of his cab and brought a policeman back to tell us that we had to agree to his new price. (I assumed that the officer would then get his cut from using his position of power to threaten us.) Reluctantly, Mr. Merryweather decided that it was not worth making a scene and he paid the extra amount.

"There's your first lesson, Miss Blake," he told me as we headed into the crowded station with more porters in tow. "Be careful and make sure about the price before you get into an Nigerian taxi."

The Train Journey

The long train, with a steam locomotive at the front of us was already waiting at the main platform for my journey to Minna, where SIM missionaries were trained for the task ahead.

"Here's your second lesson, ladies," he said as we all boarded the train. "Watch everything or it will be stolen."

As the train slowly moved out of the station, Mrs. Merryweather then regaled us with stories about thefts on the trains. "There are people who try and steal your handbag while you are asleep and at any station, who will lean through an open window and take a case." These carriages that were manufactured in England, had two classes — one for us Europeans with bunk beds — and then open coaches for the natives at the back of them. Still, though they had to put up with bad conditions there, they didn't have to pay for the trip.

After a couple of hours or so, Mr. and Mrs. Merryweather got off the train at Jebba, where they were based. With Mrs. Merryweather's warning ringing in our ears, I was afraid to go to sleep so the two us battled fatigue for the rest of the journey in the compartment we shared.

It was not long before Mr. Hummel got off and we continued on with our journey.

Just Like Bible Times

As the train flew past towns and villages, we watched the Mohammedans washing their hands and mouths before starting their prayers. They prayed five times a day. It was interesting to see these natives in their long flowing robes. It seemed to me to be just like it had been in the days of the Lord Jesus when he was on the earth. They did not seem to have changed since those days.

The miles continued to clackedy clack by and, as time progressed, I began to wonder how I would ever be able to reach these people with the Good News of Jesus Christ. Even though Nigeria had been ruled by Great Britain since 1903, there was little of the culture of my homeland in what I saw from the train. This was indeed a very foreign land.

I had studied a guide book on Nigeria as our ship had sailed there and discovered that the country was divided into three major regions marked by different cultural backgrounds. The northern Hausa-speaking area, which was largely Moslem; the Christian and Moslem Yuruba region in the south-west; and the region in the east that was dominated by the Ibo, who were overwhelmingly Christian.

I also found that the country had enormous cultural diversity, and it is estimated that there are at least 250 languages spoken in the country.

After a long night, the blood-red ball of the sun again lipped the horizon and suddenly it was day light again.

"Let's have some breakfast," I told Miss Munro, who, like me was by now red-eyed. We got out our "food box," and opened it up and brought out some food. There was a can of Libby's condensed milk, oranges, biscuits and water from a bottle.

After that, we sat at the window watching the country-side flash by. It all looked so barren and dry with not many green patches of grass about the clumps of trees. It was all burnt up by the heat. Although it was supposed to be the coolest time of the year (Harmitine) or so we were told, it felt very hot and we both used fans to try and keep cool.

The heat was at its most awful when we stopped at a station, but as soon as the train moved, it became margin-ally cooler.

We had, by now, eaten all the food given to us for the train journey that the Chief Steward packed for us, so we locked our compartment door and headed to the Dining Car. We had cold meat and salad, followed by jelly and coffee. It was very nice and cost us the equivalent of three shillings and six pence.

During the meal, the train again squealed to a halt at another station. Looking through the window, we were fas-cinated to see the natives carrying loads on their heads. Their balance was so correct. We knew we could not do it like that.

Minna Arrival

We finally arrived at Minna (it had taken nearly two days on the train, to get there from Lagos). It was about 4:00 PM in the afternoon. Several students from the language school were there on the platform to meet us and also Mrs. Marga-ret Steward, an old Redcliffite, and Mrs. Rosie Booth with her young baby in her arms. The latter was in training with me at Redcliffe and it was good to see her again. Others were there who had already finished the language study and were getting on this train to their different stations to start new work.

We were given a hearty welcome to Minna, which was also a military settlement with barracks for Army, Airforce and the colonial police. I soon discovered that the majority of the trainee missionaries were American, Canadian, Dutch and from New Zealand, though I did meet Miss Sylvia Hine, who was English. She was from Oxford and I had met her at an SIM conference some time before. We soon became firm friends.

Miss Munro and Miss Haney were told by Mrs. Steward, the hostess for the quarters, that we were to share a room on the first floor of the student quarters. It was not too far to walk from the SIM missionary station. The house in which we were quartered, looked like a mouth organ, two rows of rooms, one up and one down with a verandah between. It was made of wood and corrugated iron.

They were building a thatched school room nearby for language study as it was so hot in the sun.

On arrival at the house we were given a welcome cup of hot tea, our first for two days, and it tasted good. Mrs. Steward, our hostess, talked about her time at Redcliffe and we had a chat about the training we had received. I liked her so much and felt very much at home.

They were a mixed crowd, but were all very likable and seemed to get on well together.

By this time, the carriers had arrived with the luggage carrying it on their heads. I thought to myself that these people must be strong to carry such heavy burdens.

We unpacked what was needed and then three of us decided to go for a walk up the hill to test our "land legs" on the incline of the hill. Besides myself, there was Miss Munro and Mr. Duane Owens, who had also traveled from England on the same boat.

Supper was at 7:00 PM., and was followed by prayers held on the verandah and then to bed.

Both Miss Munro and myself slept well after the long journey. The next day, Sunday, there was to be a service in the local Hausa language held, after breakfast, at 7:30 AM., in the SIM church. This was followed with an open air meeting and testimony time from the Nigerian boys joining with us students in telling how Christ had come into our lives. It was a time of inspiration to me.

Language School

Each morning at 7:00 AM, the Christian natives would hold a prayer meeting on the grounds. Then, in the evening, the missionaries would have theirs after supper, along with hymn singing, testimony and a time of prayer before retiring.

On the Monday morning after our arrival, I went into Minna to buy a Hausa dictionary at the SIM bookshop there. I did an hour and a half study that day. I found the language study in Minna most interesting and exciting.

Each morning Mr. Steward would give us an exercise from the Hausa grammar, then at 11:00 AM., we would break for a cup of tea. After this was over, we would go to a nearby village to try out what we had learned.

It wasn't all smooth sailing, as we soon discovered. One day a student introduced my friend as a goat (Ga Akweata). She should have said, (Ga Abweata), which means "See my friend."

Of course, the people laughed and she wondered why. She asked Mr. Steward next morning in the lesson where she had gone wrong and he explained the nuance of the language. We never forgot the difference between "my friend" and "my goat". They sounded so much the same. Mr. Steward explained, "You introduced her as your goat. Why shouldn't they laugh?"

One day we were taken shopping by the wife of one of the local police working in Minna. We learned the words for meat, salt and pepper. Many other words we wrote down in a note book - both in Hausa and English.

One African lady asked us, "Abinchi ya ki" meaning "What food will you buy?" But my friend and I thought they were wanting us to buy shoes. The policeman's wife explained that we were not buying but just with her. We had many a laugh over our mistakes.

One evening, I asked Adamum, the house boy, to bring us some drinking water. We were so surprised when he arrived with a Zinc-bath full of water. It was so funny.

"I don't fancy trying to drink that water," I told Miss Munro. I later discovered that I had used the word for bath instead of drink. We were slowly learning by our linguistic slip ups!

A Bike Ride

After several weeks, a crate arrived with my beloved bicycle inside. I would not have to walk so much now. Each night, after supper, I would get on my bike and cycle around the area.

A snake appeared on the compound one day but the house boy killed it before it did any damage. Had it bitten anyone they would have died within twenty four hours. So we learned to be careful where we would tread and to shake our shoes or boots before putting them on as there might be a snake inside.

We had to ask the house boy to clean the room on Saturdays. We said, "Ka share dikina" - "Sweep my room." He would answer "Yes" in English, but would not return to do it. It was very amusing, but also extremely maddening. Eventually he understood us and then would get busy with the task at hand.

During the heat of the day, we were allowed one hours' rest. The sun was too hot, 102 to 104 degrees in the shade. We had to keep this rule for our health's sake.

After the morning service, a few of us would gather the children and hold a service for the local people using St. John's Gospel, chapter 14, verse 6. "Yesu yache, Ni ne hannya, Ni ne Gsakiya, Ni ne Rai" - "Jesus said. 'I Am the way, the truth and the life....'" Then we would hold up a picture of Jesus. They loved pictures.

As the days were passing by, I was beginning to grasp more words and sentences in the Hausa language. We used to take turns speaking to the English school held at the barracks and also speaking to the African students in Hausa.

One day, a missionary, Miss Baxter, took me to see Shafu, a blind boy living in another compound. Over the weeks, I tried to teach him Braille. I felt that I was getting somewhere at last. He was not very bright but was feeling the raised letters of the alphabet with the help of one of the head men of Minna.

We had study in the school 10 to 12 noon followed by lunch. Then followed rest from 1:00 until 2:00 PM. At 3:00 PM., a Moslem Mallam (teacher) came to instruct us. My Mallam fell asleep during the lesson and I could not awake him. He did not understand any English and I knew very little Hausa. I looked in my dictionary for a word, "Sunana samana" - "The sun is in the heavens."

I leaned forward and yelled this phrase into his ear Eventually, he awoke with a start, explaining, that it was their Ramadan fast and that he had been up all night. They did not eat during the day. He was sorry. However it was comforting to know that the fast would soon be over and they would be back to normal. This fast lasted a month.

At the end of the fast, they made a sacrifice. Each man would slit the throat of a ram, according to their custom, and offered it up to Allah. The Moslems were dressed in their best long flowing robes, as this was a special occasion.

This celebration did not make any difference to our church service. It was packed to capacity for the Breaking of Bread. It was inspiring to see the devotion of the Nigerian Christians to their Lord, in spite of the incessant noise of the beating drums outside. We listened to the speaker with rapt attention.

I visited Shafu the blind boy again and read to him from St. John's Gospel, chapter four. It was good practice for me. I managed to give him a short message from it. We always sang choruses during these visits, and the natives would stand around and some would even join in. I would give Shafu a lesson in Braille from the lesson book. He seemed to be keen to learn more and his touch was improving and every day he began to read a little more.

I wrote to the blind girls, Edna, Nancy and Laura, from the Blind School in Liverpool, to tell them about Shafu's progress.

* * * * *

Five weeks had passed and it was now Christmas Eve. I was soon to discover that in Nigeria, it was not universally celebrated like in England. In Minna, only the Christians (native believers) observed it. I spent part of the time writing letters to England. Then we went over to the European Club in the town, to put presents on the tree there and sing Christmas Carols with the other ex-patriots.

Christmas Day dawned, I was so disappointed at not being able to go to church. I had a bad nose bleed (this happened often) and so had to lay down on my bed. I was so disappointed to not be at the service.

After a few hours, my problem cleared up and I was able to join the others for a special tea, followed by some games. There was a sudden rustle in the trees and Father Christmas (Santa Claus) arrived in the form of Mr. Ray Dalahay, a Canadian missionary. Resplendent in a red robe and white beard he handed out the presents to all of us. The children of the missionaries and the native kids particularly enjoyed that part of it.

However, three of the African boys ran away at first, frightened by his red cloak. It reminded them of the Juju man. They soon got over the fright. It was a great time for all of us.

Supper was at 7:00 p.m.. After that we sat outside and sang around the log fire until it was time for bed.

The next day I took Miss Seal, an American, to the village and the children came running to us. They wanted to hear more stories about Jesus. They sang, "Yes, Jesus loves me" (I Yana sonmu). There were about 40 children listening. They sang many action choruses and learned verses of scripture, St. John 3:16, 14:6. We closed in prayer. We held these meetings often as it helped us with our language. I was beginning to speak quite well. I helped Miss Seal with Hausa and this taught her more and gave her more confidence to try and speak.

I visited a Moslem compound every week to speak to the wives living there. One day, we arrived on the day of sacrifice and were allowed to watch the ceremony. Each man would slit the throat of a ram for his house and then one was killed on the hill for the sin of the people and for the head Moslem himself.

I always took my Braille writing board and dotter with me as it would give me openings with people that I saw under a tree. I would draw a crowd as soon as I began writing on the slate. They would come over to watch me writing Braille. While they watched I told them the Good News of the Gospel.

I was taken to see one of the chief Moslems. He tried to barter for (buy) the Braille board. He said he would give me his Moslem slate for it? He wrote prayers on his slate for people, then would wash them off with water and put the water into a vessel for payment, saying, "Whoever drinks this water will keep well." I had my doubts about his claims, but refrained from saying my thoughts so as not to offend.

One day it was arranged that the students at Minna would go to another community called Piko. Some went by car, the rest on bikes. I was one of the latter and enjoyed it very much. We stayed in a large round hut, one big room with a large verandah around it. I slept on the verandah with Miss Whitmore.

The chief and some of his men came out to greet us and brought corn and chicken and asked if we would go and preach in his village. We were warmly welcomed. We sang choruses, and hymns, then played the gramophone (record player). Our Christian native boys came with us to help.

The local people lived high in the rocks away from the enemy, as in times gone by they were hunted down by the people of the North who burnt their villages and took the people as slaves. About 50 people sat around the gramophone (record player) It was such an attraction. They were so fascinated by it, they sat and listened. They joined in the singing. Even the chief enjoyed it and gave us a large bunch of bananas.

We eventually had our language exam results and I had passed. So I started packing my things to go to Miango where I was to spend a month's vacation.

The Wooding family pictured in Liverpool, England, in the mid 1940s. Left to right: Ruth, Alfred, Dan and Anne.

Alf and Anne Wooding in their beloved Merseyside during their retirement.

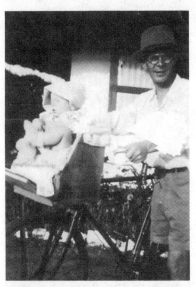

Alf with "Dan Juma" on the front of his bicycle as he sets out to evangelize the local villages with the help of the blue-eyed baby.

Anne with "Dan Juma" and Baba at the SIM Miango rest home.

Alf Wooding complete with his baggy pants in Nigeria.

Some of "Dan Juma's" playmates in Nigeria — Jumper, Ungaloo and Juma.

The "Happy Day." Alf and Anne pictured outside the church in Kano after their wedding.

Ann with "Dan Juma" on the front of her bicycle.

Anne and Alf Wooding after their wedding

One of the Nigerian helpers takes "Dan Juma" for a walk.

Anne Wooding (center) is surrounded by her family after the funeral of Alf. Left to right: Peter, Sharon, Andrew, Ruth, Norma, Allen Ross (Aunt Lottie's grandson) and Dan.

Friends and family gather after the funeral service for Alf Wooding at New Brighton Baptist Church in England. Anne Wooding is center (front) with Norma and Dan Wooding next to her. Front far right is Dennis Stevens with his wife Margaret. They followed Alf and Anne to Nigeria to work as SIM missionaries. Far left (front) is John Miles with his wife Grace next to him. They now run REAP International and live in the home where the Woodings once lived in FeatherstoneRoad, Birmingham, England.

Chapter Ten

THE WALLED CITY

After our time at Miango, each of us language students were then sent to the various stations appointed to us. My assignment was to go to probably the most absorbing city in the whole of Nigeria — the famed walled city of Kano in the north, located on the edge of the vast Sahara desert.

"Nancy, we want you to help pioneer a work among the blind Moslem men of Kano," I was told by Mrs. Bingham, Roland Bingham's wife. "This city has been closed to us so far, but we are going to see if the Emir (king) of Kano would let us send you and others in there to teach the unsighted men to read and write in Hausa.

My expertise in Braille was the reason why I was given this unusual mission field.

It was then that my old insecurities began to surface, as I wondered if I would be able to cope with the language. I was fluent in English, Braille, but Hausa; I wasn't so sure if I would be able to cope. I was already finding it an extremely difficult language to master, and I knew that to translate it

79

then into the language of dots, would be even more diffi-cult. No English at all was spoken in Kano, so this would be a whole new challenge for me.

I traveled there by train on January 6 1939, with three Canadian partners, Miss Seal, Miss Fiona Kibby and Miss Susan Sneck.

It soon became obvious to me that this was a completely different region. The dry climate produced grasses, stunted shrubs, acacias and other drought-resistant plants that could survive the meager or variable rainfall.

We passed by nomads who used the grasslands as pas-ture for their herds of beef cattle. They had chosen this area, I was later told, because it was free of the cattle-killing tsetse flies.

The further north we went, it was even more noticeable that the soil quality had declined and desert conditions had spread making everywhere quite barren.

The War Clouds

We were all aware that the war clouds were gathering in Europe as Adolf Hitler's Nazi war machine was beginning to cause panic there. Still, in this far flung part of the British Empire, people seemed oblivious to where Hitler's saber rattling was going to lead. We would soon discover that the little Austrian house-painter would be painting Europe's battle fields with blood.

Dr. Albert Helser met us at Kano station and he drove us to the nearby SIM mission station. There we were warmly welcomed by the resident missionaries and we enjoyed our first day with them. Dr. Helser and his wife Lola were very lovely people to be with. I knew that I was going to be happy with these folks. Miss Kibby and I were to work to-gether teaching the blind.

Miss Kibby had arrived from Ethiopia after all the mis-sionaries there had been sent out of that country by

Mussolini, the strutting black-shirt leader of Italy. "Il Duche" (The Leader), had taken possession of this land in 1935 and Emperor Haile Selassie, who was named regent in 1916 and subsequently crowned emperor in 1930, had fled the country and was now in hiding in England hoping one day to return to his country.

Miss Kibby and I shared a room with a bathroom and toilet. We got to know each other well.

One day Bate, a blind boy, came to join us, from a bush station called Bununu, where he had been living with his family. After he was led to a deep faith in the Lord by a missionary, he had learned the basics of Hausa Braille and had felt the call of God to full time service to teach the blind.

Every day he learned a little more. Bate enjoyed writing as that was something new to him. He was quick to learn and eager to give to teach the blind.

"I wanted to be useful instead of begging for a living," he told me one day. "I also want to tell these people about the Lord Jesus Christ and to witness to His saving and keeping power."

He became my first student in Kano. I was charged with helping him further his Braille reading and teaching him to write with the Braille board and dotter. He was eager to give his testimony to all with whom he came in contact. He also preached in the Sudan Interior Church on Sundays. The local people would marvel at a blind man being able to do so many things.

The Emir of Kano

Now that we were ready to start our ministry in Kano, Dr. Helser managed to secure an interview with the Emir of Kano. He took Bate along with him. This king of about 500,000 Moslem people, was interested to see what could be done for the thousands of blind people of his domain.

In his spectacular palace, the Emir examined Bate's work, including the mat and hat he had made. He also tested his reading and writing abilities and he passed with flying colors. The Emir's face lit up like a lamp as he watched Bate's nimble fingers flying over the writing board and dotter. He was very impressed. This led him to give his permission to teach the blind in the old city.

"I will lay down one condition, however," he told Dr. Helser. "You must not preach your religion unless you are asked about it."

He then called one of his hovering servants to bring him his seal and he wrote on the document it was affixed to that he gave us his authorization to work in the city.

The great day came for us to go to the main gate of the walled city. The city had sixteen entrances in all, and guards were on duty at each. No one was allowed entry without the Emir's permission. The uniformed guard carefully checked the seal and writing and eventually allowed Miss Kibby, Bate, Barko (our house boy) and myself to pass through.

On entering the city, I was reminded of the walls of Jericho. There were high walls all around their city with tunneled entrances with houses built into the walls. As we went into the city, I noticed that the houses were all made of mud and had flat roofs, the roads were sandy and very dry as they only have rain for one month in the whole year. It seemed to me that this city had not changed for centuries.

Waiting for us on horseback were two of the leaders of Kano, the Alkawi (the title given to a ruler.) They bowed and saluted from a great height in their long flowing robes. My friends and I felt very privileged and saluted them.

On either side of the road sat beggars. Many were blind and deaf and some were grotesquely maimed. They would wait until we were passing and say, "In sadeka sebilda Mohamadin Allah"? - (Where is your gift because of the prophet of God?). The whole scene was, to me, just like a picture out of the Old Testament.

We were then escorted to a section of the city where only blind people lived. When we arrived there, the sighted and elderly Chief with a long beard, greeted us and insisted on being our first student.

"My people must see that I have been taught before they will listen to you," he explained.

My heart dropped when I heard this.

"This is terrible," I muttered to myself. "I don't think he has any hope of learning Braille?"

Still, we had no option but to try and teach him the intricacies of Braille. Surprisingly, he quickly picked up the rudiments and, after he had learned a little, he gathered the blind people together to explain why we were there.

"These persons have come to teach you how to read and write," he told the assembled group.

After they had heard this, they were all eager to start. After a briefing, we told them to come back the next day and we would start the lessons.

Under the Mango Tree

The blind people gathered together there under the cooling branches of a large mango tree for the first lesson.

We began to go there every day from 10:00 a.m. to 12:00 noon. The guards began to know us as each day we arrived just before 10:00 a.m. Barko would be riding on the tandem with Bate on the cross-bar and Miss Kibby on the back. The natives would stand and stare at the three of them as they arrived on this strange form of transportation.

After a few days, The Chief allowed us to rent a house with two rooms. Dr. Jericho and others helped to tar and whitewash the place and put mats on the floors. It all looked very clean. So each day we held school in this facility.

The school soon began to grow in numbers. I watched with joy as they gingerly began to feel the embossed letters of the alphabet.

News soon spread about what we were doing and Moslem teachers came around to find out what was going on. They were amazed that a blind boy could read. Sadly on September 3 1939, war broke out and the world was plunged into chaos.

Bate continued with the good work on the missionary compound. Eventually an eye specialist came to the hospital that was built there. Many people received their sight. Bate started a school for those who did not receive their sight. He had the joy of leading many of them to Christ. So our labors were not in vain at Kano. Bate became a wonderful teacher of the Bible and preached regularly at the Kano church.

As hate began to envelope the world, love came into mine in the form of Alf Wooding. Another chapter of my life was about to begin.

Chapter Eleven

LOVE — AFRICAN STYLE

I t was while I was at language school in Minna that I first met Alf Wooding, a slightly built man with a broad smile, brown, curly hair and circular glasses. Like the other male missionaries, he also had on short, baggy pants.

"Would you like to see the *Liverpool Echo*?" he said as he held up my home-town newspaper and then came and sat at a dining table with me. "It's just arrived."

I was very surprised to see the paper and gratefully took it from him. He then delivered another shock to me.

"Nancy, you probably don't remember me, but I was at your farewell meeting at Donaldson Street on November 1, 1937," he revealed. "I had been accepted by SIM for service here after graduating from the Bible Training Institute in Glasgow, and I heard about you from one of the SIM staff.

"I was really moved by your testimony and I hoped that we could meet once I arrived."

Following in His Brother's Footsteps

It was now six months later, and Alf had recently made the same journey as I from Liverpool and was just beginning his language studies. "I'm from Toxteth," he went on. "I'm following in my brother Will's footsteps. He's already working with the Fulani people of the north with SIM. He's married to a lovely girl called Margaret."

Before I could say anything, this charming man, who I realized was the student that Miss Munro had alluded to on the ship, pressed on with his story. "My brother led me to the Lord and encouraged me to get trained before coming to Nigeria," he stated. "I can't tell you how happy I am to be here at last."

Alf's easy manner and Liverpool humor, made him instantly attractive to me, but I also knew that I had not come to Africa to find a husband, but to rather work as a missionary to the blind.

We had been alone in the room when Mego, one of the natives, came in. He had obviously been sent by one of the other missionaries to keep an eye on us.

Alf tried to ignore the hovering figure and asked me how much longer I would be in Minna.

"I've just got one more written exam to take and then, if I pass, I'll be posted to Kano," I told him.

He rubbed his chin and then stated, "Well, that doesn't give us much time to get to know each other."

I said nothing, so he added, "Let's go for a little walk in the grounds. I could do with some fresh air."

It was now getting towards dusk and the cooling winds, I knew, would be refreshing. With that, he led the way to the door and, under a beautiful crescent moon standing proudly in the center of thousands of ruby stars, I followed him as Mego stood rooted to the spot, not quite sure what his next move should be.

I smiled at the African and he got the message that he should not follow us. The air was rent with grunts and whistles, yet no birds or animals came near.

"A little bit different than Liverpool," Alf chortled as he smashed a mosquito that had landed on his forearm. "Not too many of these in Everton!"

I smiled, but again stood there, feeling awkward. Here I was with a man whom I had just met and yet already had begun to feel attracted to. I was not sure how I should act. This was not a subject that had been taught to me at Redcliffe or here at the language school.

A Kiss at Dusk

Without warning, Alf suddenly took a step forward and took me in his arms and planted a kiss on my lips. He held it for a long moment and then stopped. I stood rooted to the ground, my heart pounding mercilessly. The clammy heat wrapped itself around me, bathing my body in sweat. I mopped my face awkwardly with my handkerchief.

"You don't waste any time, Alf Wooding," I said.

"Well, we don't have much time, do we?" he responded, again a smile blooming on his face. "I understand that you will be leaving soon and so I wanted you to know how I felt about you.

"I liked you from the very first moment I saw you at Donaldson Street. I've been planning that kiss all the way across the Atlantic."

The next day, I was standing on a ladder in the mission church, painting a scripture scroll in English, Hausa and Yoruba on the wall when I heard the sound of footsteps and turned around to see the slight figure of Alf approaching.

"So, you're an artist as well as a linguist," he said.

"Alf, I hope you are going to behave yourself this time round," I responded. "After all, we are in church."

He ignored my barbed remark and just stood there. "Don't let me hold you up," he said. "I just wanted to see your handiwork."

I felt my hand tremble just a little as I tried to continue with my work. He remained silent for a few minutes, and then pulled a camera from behind his back, and took a picture of me as I completed the task.

"I'll see you later, Nancy Blake," he said as he then left me.

A couple of hours later, I was in the town center with Shefu, the blind boy I had been teaching, and once again the little man with the big camera appeared on the scene. We were there for Shefu to show me around the colorful market and, before we knew it, the loud click of the shutter was heard startling the natives standing by.

"What is the white man doing?" one of them asked.

"He's capturing the spirit of the white woman," another responded, having seen a black and white photograph.

Each day, we would see each other, but I knew that it could not last, because I had, by now, passed by my last exam and was due to leave for Kano, and my work with the blind people of that historic walled city.

When we said good-bye, Alf looked very sad. "I'll write to you all the time," he promised. "And, next time we meet, I'll give you another copy of the *Echo*."

He was true to his word, and the letters just kept coming. I would rip open each envelope eagerly and read about how his lessons were coming along and then, when I had a spare moment, I would pen a reply.

"Alf, life is very different here," I told him in one epistle. "It's very dry here and the people are mostly Moslems. I am hoping soon to be able to start a work along with some of my colleagues with the blind men of the city."

One letter caused me to become excited. "Nancy, I am coming to see you," it said. "I need to talk to you urgently about something important."

Dr. Helser, the superintendent of the Kano station, took me in his car to Kano Station to meet Alf. We arrived just in time for the huge steam locomotive to chug into the platform and Alf soon disembarked. He cut a dashing figure in his pith helmet and smart white shirt and shorts.

We shook hands — we could not do anything else with Dr. Helser standing there — and then we all headed back for the mission station.

After being introduced to the other missionaries and then being shown his quarters, Alf came to the dining room and invited me to take a walk with him.

"I'm afraid we can't be alone, this time," I explained. "They want Baba, the house boy, to accompany us."

Alf smiled to himself. "I have a plan," he said. "I know how I can get rid of him."

Animal Sounds

As we began to walk around the grounds, Baba walking a few steps behind us, Alf suddenly cupped his lips and made the sound of a hyena. With that, the startled African turned on his heels, and ran towards the main house.

With that, Alf again leaned forward and kissed me. "I've really missed you, Nancy," he then said. "I decided that letters were just not good enough. We really have to spend some time together."

I then shocked him by asking where my *Liverpool Echo* was.

"Don't worry," he said. "I've got a copy with me in my room. But I think we have more important ...."

His voice trailed off as Baba reappeared. Again Alf cupped his mouth and made the sound of the hyena. Baba once more ran away, and we were alone for a few more minutes.

I had to give Alf full marks for tenacity. He was not going to allow distance and a house boy to come between us.

During his short visit, I spent most of the day, learning Hausa Braille and we would only see each other during the meal periods. As soon as the meal bell went, he would stand at the door for me to arrive and then accompany me to a table. The other missionaries knew what was going on and would leave us alone to continue our "courtship."

Alf, in between eating the food that was being served, would tell me more about his life in Liverpool.

I discovered that he had attended a small mission hall and had an equal fire to myself in feeling God's call to Nigeria.

Wee Alfie

"I really enjoyed my time in Scotland," he told me one evening. "The other students even Christened me 'Wee Alfie.' I can't imagine why?"

I joined him in laughter. But I knew that his small figure contained a huge heart for the Lord. We not only had the same Liverpool accent, but we also had the same faith in Jesus Christ.

Alf had, by now, passed all his language exams, and had been sent to Izom, to work with mainly pagan people of the area.

Before he left, I was summoned to Dr. Helser's office for a chat. "Nancy," he told me as I took a seat across the desk from him, "we have all been discussing your relationship with Alf."

My heart sank as I expected him to rule that we could no longer be friends.

"Nancy," he started up again, "we think that you are both suited for each other and we also believe that you should get engaged."

I could hardly believe my ears.

"We think that you and Alf should spend a few moments together so he can propose to you," he said, a smile appearing on his face from ear to ear.

With that, he indicated that I should go and find Alf and tell him the news. "And this time I promise that Baba will not be around," he added.

Alf was all smiles when I shared with him the news. We walked to the far edge of the compound and, as the red ball of the sun sank beyond the horizon, he sank to his knees, and said, "Nancy Blake, the love of my life, will you marry me?"

I blinked back a tear of joy and replied, "Yes, of course I will."

The next day, a happy crowd of 25 of us gathered in the dining hall for our official engagement party.

The date for our wedding was to be Alf's birthday — August 27, 1939 — but it eventually took place shortly afterwards on September 5, in the Kano SIM mission church.

* * * * *

I was waiting in my bedroom, all dressed up in a beautiful white dress that had been made for me by Mrs. Harris, the wife of Dr. Harris, who was to give me away. But nobody came to tell me that it was time for me to make my grand entrance. The church was packed like sardines with people who were to witness our wedding.

I kept looking at my watch and people in the sanctuary were checking theirs.

Alf stood nervously at the front, wondering what was causing the hold up. Then he remembered that he was supposed to tell Baba to come and get me. He dispatched the house boy forthwith and soon I was waiting at the front door of the church and then the organist began playing "The Wedding March."

As I slowly walked down the aisle, with Dr. Harris at my side, carrying a bouquet of flowers, I was followed by Evelyn Dancy, 5, who was bridesmaid, and her 3-year-old brother, Walter, who was the pageboy.

Then Alf turned to look at me and nearly broke down with emotion.

The service was a blur to me, but I do remember Dr. Helser, who was officiating saying, "For better...for worse...in sickness and health."

Those words were to prove prophetic for us both. But in the excitement of the moment, I did not give them much thought.

Chapter Twelve

FIRE AND RAIN

Following a brief honeymoon at Patiga in Yoruba country, where Will and Margaret were based along with their children, Harold and Norman. Alf and I then went to his station near to Izom in a pagan area down south. We took the train to Izom, arriving during a torrential tropical rainstorm in this small town of mud huts.

When we got to our compound at 8:00 PM, we discovered that Mama, our cook, had gone home and the main house was all locked up. Baba, the house boy, was missing, and he also had a key.

"I think we had better sit under the mango tree and hope one of them comes back soon, Nan," suggested Alf, who liked to call me by that nickname.

Dark and Wet

As the rain continued to tumble out of the sky like sheets of gray metal, we found the tree offered little shelter and we were soon drenched to the skin. I had been used to a modern mission station and felt overwrought as this place looked so drab and, very lonely. Nobody was about and it was so dark. I wondered if I had done the right thing in coming here.

Seeing my expression of incredulity, Alf took my hand and assured me that all would be well. I was not so sure, but I smiled weakly at him.

Then, after a few long minutes, out of the shadows, came the dripping figure of Mama.

"Sanude zuwa, uwa Gida," (Greetings on your coming,) he said. His smiling and gentle persona made me suddenly feel at home. I liked him very much and we got on very well together. He was the cook and also the evangelist and went everywhere with us.

Mama opened the door and struck a match to light the oil lamp on a table. In the flickering shadows I squinted my eyes and could just make out that the inside was newly decorated to receive the bride. I realized that my husband had done the place up as best he could with such an old building. I decided to make the best of it.

We soon retired to bed and our first night was a very uncomfortable one, as the rain poured down all night, echoing noisily on the thatched grass roof.

Next day I felt happier when I saw another house across the muddy compound. It was dry and much better so we moved in there and just used the other one for our meals.

I had learned the Hausa language but here at Izom they spoke Bwari and I could not understand a word of what was being said by the local people. Fortunately for me, in the market, the women selling meat and vegetables, spoke Hausa. I visited the little church in Izom. This unpretentious, low ceiling mud sanctuary with wire mesh windows, was about a mile away from our home and was accessed by crossing the bridge over River Gurara that ran alongside our house.

On that first morning, I also stood by the fast-flowing waters and watched the native women wash themselves, and their pots and pans, in the murky river.

I began to feel that I was going to like it here. It took a few days before I got used to working on the menu for our meals with Mama and seeing to the water filter. Mama would bring pots full of water into the house and then we would have to thoroughly boil it until it was safe to drink.

Our First Visitor

Soon, we had our first visitor, a blind boy from Diko in his early twenties. Esther Anderson invited him to stay in the compound for a month. He did not speak the same language as the people here at Izom, but he knew the Hausa so I managed to teach him Braille reading and writing in this language. He was a Christian and very keen to learn and so, every morning, I spent an hour or two taking him through his lessons. Then, in the afternoon, he and Alf would accompany me to the SIM school in the town, where my husband and I would teach in the school. We taught in Hausa and the children soon picked up the language.

There was an extraordinary age range of students. They ranged from three to sixty years of age, and all eagerly learned the "ABC" together. The older ones found it very difficult to learn as school was something new to them.

Two of our brightest pupils were Galadima, 15, and 16-year-old Ungalu who soon began to read and received a Bible, hymn book and a copy of *Pilgrim's Progress* in Hausa from us. These were given as prizes for hard work in the class. These boys and Mama, carried their Bibles with them everywhere.

We then started a prayer meeting on the compound each morning at 7:00 AM., and these boys, and Mama, would be there on time ready to sing some hymns and pray to the Lord. It was very encouraging to hear them worshipping their Creator. The blind boy also joined them. He was used to the prayer meetings held at his own mission station at Diko.

Alf and I would rise at 5:30 AM and, after washing ourselves, we would have a "quiet time" until 6:30 AM., when we would read aloud our Bibles to each other and then sink to the side of our bed and have a time of prayer.

Then Mama would arrive and prepare the breakfast before our compound prayer meeting.

My medical training at St. Columbus Hospital came in useful and so we began a clinic for the sick people of Izom. Patients would first gather under the mango tree for a service that would begin with them singing hymns.

Mama would then preach a short sermon and then Alf left on his bicycle down dusty trails to visit local villages. Wearing the obligatory white pith helmet that most of the missionaries wore, he would stand under a tree and then speak to the people in their language, telling them the timeless story of the Gospel. He would then invite them to receive the Savior into their heart, and many would respond.

The Clinic

While he was away, I continued with the medical work. At first the people were afraid to come, having been warned by the witch doctor that we were practicing "bad juju." These evil practitioners of the black arts, were worried that we would take business away from them.

However, whenever the witch doctor went away to other towns and villagers, they were not afraid and came to the compound in large numbers. When others saw that these patients were getting better in health through the treatment, they would come also for me to treat their ailments.

I had a government permit to give treatment to the natives and had established a dispensary on the compound. The patients would be given water with disinfectant in it and swabs of cotton wool to clean their sores as most of them had ulcers. Then I would look at them and treat accordingly. When that was finished I would close the dispensary and begin teaching the blind boy for an hour or so and, in between that, I would see Mama about the meals for the day while Baba, the other boy, would do the housework and make the bed.

A Snake on the Roof

We also had Tagway, who looked after the compound. He would use a scythe to keep the grass down to avoid the danger of poisonous snakes hiding in it and then getting into the house before we could see them. Despite his valiant efforts, one fell from the roof right in front of us as we stepped out of the house. We knew that it had to be killed or it would have killed us with its poisonous venom. One of the native boys took a stick and hacked it to death.

"It must have been in the old thatched roof of the house," said Alf as we breathed a sigh of relief.

In the future, we were extremely careful to watch out for them when we were at the old house for our meals.

By now, we had moved into the dry season, and during one market day, some of the natives deliberately set a fire to the brush close to our home, to force out animals that had been hiding there, so they could kill and eat them. The bush fire jumped onto the old thatched roof and, in a split second, was ablaze. It was a very frightening experience for us as we helplessly watched our home begin to burn down.

People came from the market to help put it out with buckets of water from the river, but it was all in vain, and the house just kept on burning like an inferno.

To add to this appalling situation, some of our items, including our old wind-up gramophone, were stolen that day by natives as they helped carry out our property. They were supposed to be rescuing the goods, but then made off with them. Later we were told that the thieves were glee-fully playing records in another part of the town, as we tried to deal with the traumatic loss of our home.

Alf and I were up all night in case the fire caught the other house. Eventually the inferno died down and we went inside the charred shell of the house to examine the walls. We discovered that they were about to collapse after being eaten away by white ants.

"I guess that the fire saved us having to pull the house down," said Alf, with a wry sense of humor. "Otherwise, we would eventually have had to demolish it and start from scratch."

We never wanted to see another fire like that.

A Generous Donor

We moved into the original house and began to ask God how we could possible tear down the old house and then rebuild a new one in its place.

Eventually, an elderly lady in England, who was a SIM supporter and whose name we never discovered, heard of the need of a house at Izom and so donated 80 pounds (ster-ling) to help us purchase the goods to rebuild it. So we be-gan to make plans to build. We commissioned some of the local people to go down the river by boat and find enough large stones and rocks for us to start the foundation.

We hired a brick layer and a carpenter to do the special work and local laborers and a drummer to keep them happy. (Africans always work better when there is a rhythm to do their tasks to.)

These men would work while we watched them, but when you turned your back, they would sit and do nothing until you returned, but still expected to be paid just the same. Alf taught them how to make bricks and they would leave them in the sun for several days to dry.

Finally, after six long months, our house was completed and we liked it very much. For those 80 pounds, we also had an extra guest house constructed for visitors That was in 1940 and we had many visitors, especially Nigerian and British soldiers whose trucks had broken down on the road.

The Gold Mine

Mr. Francis, an Englishman who ran a gold mine about 40 miles from Izom toward Minna, often would invite Alf and myself, to be his guests for a fortnight (two weeks) to hold meetings for the African miners to get them "converted" as he did not trust the unconverted as they used to steal his gold.

We enjoyed our stay. We were living in luxury for those two weeks and some of the natives were converted. He had several Christians working for him and they were delighted to help us with services. We were trying to convert the miner but he would not listen.

We had fresh meat and milk. A thing in the past for my husband and me. We only had fresh milk one month of the year.

Mr. Francis built a church in the village for the men and their families to go on Sundays hoping to get more Christians. His mining town was very clean and well kept and he ruled over it as a king over his kingdom.

The Christians there would hold prayer meetings and pray for the owner's soul. Then they would hand him a tract to read about salvation. He would draw a circle in the dust of the ground with heaven in the middle saying all roads led to heaven but he did not trust the other one. We had the meetings several times a year. It was a real holiday for me.

We were living what seemed to be a million miles from the war with Germany. As Hitler's troops were advancing on all fronts and nightly bombing London, something exciting was beginning to occur within me. I was pregnant with our first child.

Chapter Thirteen

"DAN-JUMA"

As I lay in bed, listening to the eerie whistling of night birds and the distant howling of hyenas intruding into the still night air, I grimaced and then smiled as I felt the baby inside of me kick violently.

I leaned over and gently shook Alf who was, by now, in a deep slumber. "Sorry to wake up you," I said as he stirred. "But I think it's getting close. Maybe, we should start making preparations for the trip to Vom Hospital."

We had agreed that having the baby in Izom might be dangerous, for if any problems arose, there would be no one there who could help with the situation.

On a previous visit to Vom, I had talked with Dr. Percy Barnden, a British missionary doctor with the Sudan United Mission, and he had agreed with my prognosis.

"When you think the time is close, Nan, try to get here and I will deliver your child for you," he had promised.

But the predicament was that the hospital was a long distance away. This was not Britain, where it would be possible to go direct there by modern transportation.

101

To add to the complication, the former Austrian house painter, Adolf Schicklgruber (Hitler) was trying to take over the world — just as my first-born was struggling to get into it. This had even affected Nigeria, where all petrol (gasoline) was now rationed.

"Maybe the mail truck, on its way to Minna, will be passing by later today," Alf suggested, knowing that this was just a vain hope. "If it does, you could ride on it and then catch the train to Vom."

As the moonless dark of that December night in 1940 was being replaced by the early-morning rays of the run, we started to make preparations for my long journey.

After a couple of hours, all was packed, but there was still no sign of any transportation and, again, I felt a "kick" inside of me.

The Only Hope

We were beginning to get anxious about the situation and so Alf and I sank to our knees at the side of our bed and prayed that God would urgently send assistance.

I guess we had not expected to receive an immediate answer to our prayer. After all, to see a car pass by our home was a thrill, but it was a seldom experienced one.

As we got to our feet, we heard the sound of a car drawing into the compound. We both ran outside to see who it was. A chauffeur got out at the door and I recognized that he worked for the miner.

"Hello, Mrs. Wooding," he said brightly. "My boss thought you might need a ride to Minna. He's got some extra rations of fuel and guessed you might be close to having the baby and asked me to come and collect you."

We were both totally astonished with his visit. He had come 40 miles out of his way to pick me up. I gathered up my items and kissed Alf good-bye.

Baba, the house boy, was roused and told that he would accompany me on the trip. He packed his roll-up bed, and we got into the car.

The man then drove back to the mine, where Mr. Francis got into the car with an empty trunk that he was to pack with food for himself and his staff from Minna. He would not take any payment for the fuel.

We stayed over night at the SIM station in Minna. Early next morning, the driver took Baba and myself to the railway station. It was Baba's first train journey. He was very excited, also afraid of loosing me as he was not allowed to stay with me on the excursion. Nigerian Railways, in those days, did not allow Africans and Europeans to share carriages.

So, every time the train stopped, Baba would dash along the platform to see if I was still on the train.

As the train pulled into the station, located in the Jos plateau, and screeched to a halt, I spotted the familiar figure of Dr. Barnden waiting on the platform. He took us to Vom hospital in his car.

After a time there, the labor pains began and then, after a further eight hours of struggle, my first-born son, Daniel Tanswell Wooding, arrived bawling and spluttering.

"You've got a boy, Anne," said the doctor, as he snipped his umbilical cord and then slapped a mosquito that was probing his arm. That miracle of birth had taken place on Thursday, December 19, 1940.

I smiled gently as I looked down at my child and then took him in my arms as Dr. Barnden handed the mite to me.

* * * * *

Alf was anxiously waiting in our mud-walled home in Izom, for news of the birth. A telephone call from the hospital to the British government outpost in Abuja (now the Nigerian capital), announced my birth. Then an African messenger walked 30 miles to Izom to tell Alf the good news. The messenger finally arrived on Friday, December 20.

"You have a son," beamed the exhausted courier to a background of bleating goats, barking dogs and shouting boys.

A cheer broke out among the many natives, as they crowded into the small Wooding compound. They laughed, danced and clapped their hands. Alf smiled, pride showing in his eyes. Now, he knew, would come the traditional naming ritual.

"We must call him 'Dan-Juma,' which means Son of Friday," said one of the natives, dressed only in a loin cloth.

"Yes," the others chorused. "He is to be 'Dan-Juma.'"

Talking Drums

Much tongue-clacking greeted the new name. The "resolution" had been unanimously carried, and so Alf decided not to tell them that our son had, in fact, been born not on Friday, but Thursday. Talking drums quickly spread the news that "Dan-Juma" had arrived.

Alf packed a few belongings for the long trip to Vom, which included being able to "hitch a ride" on the mail truck to Minna — a journey of 24 hours — and then the long rail journey to Vom.

It was Christmas Eve when the slight figure of my husband hurried into the ward to meet his little, gurgling son for the first time. The child looked up into his father's weather-beaten open face, with no idea how this courageous man from Liverpool had obeyed God's call and left his home to bring the gospel to the sweltering land where millions had still not heard of Jesus Christ. Where tribe after tribe had been caught in the bonds of animism, witchcraft and ancestral worship, while millions had already turned to Islam.

As I gathered my strength, we went to Miango Rest House for a months' holiday. I spent the first part of the month in bed as I was not too strong after the baby arrived. My husband had to look after the baby. He bathed Daniel every day. Sue Hoagie, a nurse, would come to also take care of the baby, but when Alf saw her approaching, he would send her off, wanting this role exclusively for himself. So she did general nursing for me until I was allowed up.

After the month was up we returned with "Dan-Juma," to the dusty village of Izom, a cluster of mud huts crowded with grass roofs. The natives were delighted to see him and gave us a real welcome home. They had never seen a blue-eyed white baby before, so he became quite a celebrity in the community.

The Blue-Eyed Meal Ticket

Many Moslems lived in the community and one of them, an old chief, was soon to provide us with a meal ticket. As our son lay in a cot in a temperature of 110 degrees Fahrenheit in the shade, he swept into our hut, and welcomed us. As he grinned, he revealed a few orange-stained teeth that had survived his 73 years of life.

Alf got out a grass mat for him to squat on and then the chief issued an order to me.

"White woman," he gestured grandly, "I have some more gifts for you and the 'little white god.' But first I have a request."

"Yes Chief," I replied, as I anxiously eyed the bananas, eggs and the four live, struggling chickens his bearers were holding.

"You must bathe him for me."

I knew that this little favor would help replenish our dwindling food stocks. He was, for some reason, fascinated to see our "little white god" cleansed of all the clinging dust of Nigeria.

"You must also give me sweet tea with Carnation milk in it," he added.

The tea was served and then the strapping figure of Mama, filled a bowl of water and then I proceeded to pour a calabash of water over the baby, time and time again.

The chief had come on several occasions to observe this strange ritual. This was different from washing as he understood it. His large collection of children and grandchildren from his three wives were usually unceremoniously dipped in the pale-green waters of the nearby Guarara River.

As I bathed "Dan-Juma," his face, a dark map of wrinkles, beamed with happiness. The smoky fire that was used to cook upon, cast dancing shadows across the room

After it was over, he ordered one of his servants to "prepare the gifts." He handed them to Mama, who was forced to chase after those of the chickens that had escaped the attentions of the chief's man. After grabbing these squawking creatures, he wrung their scraggy necks.

"Okay," said the head man to Alf, "now I have given you a gift, you must give me one in return."

My husband fished about the pockets of his baggy pants and finally found an English silver shilling and handed over the coin to the chief. With that the ceremony of "appeasing the child god" was over; all parties bowed, the chief left as quickly as he had arrived, and our eardrums continued to buzz with the sound of mosquitoes.

* * * * *

"The White-Man's Religion"

Mama became a crowning jewel to us. The local witch doctor was so angry with his conversion that he poisoned his food saying that he had taken the "white man's religion." But after three attempts, Mama did not die so the witch doctor concluded that he must be a god, so he left him alone.

Mama was not only our cook, but also helped us in evangelism. He would travel with us and carry us across the steams and then go back for the bicycles. He was strong, well-built and fearless.

But even Mama was not the draw to bring in the crowds that "Dan-Juma" was.

Chapter Fourteen

THE WISDOM OF SOLOMON

The going had been tough in our outreach to the people of Izom — until the birth of "Dan-Juma." That changed everything. We were welcomed into the community as "Dan-Juma" became a real draw. The natives never tired of calling on us to see him and bring presents. There was an abundant supply of eggs, bananas, yams and scraggy chickens. We never went hungry after that.

Alf would strap the baby into a little wooden chair on the front of his upright bicycle and they would bump down seemingly endless dusty trails through nine-foot high grass on either side that concealed many dangers — from snakes to quiet, watching monkeys. He would constantly ring the bike's bell to frighten off the wildlife and would be greeted in return by the racket of exotic birds over his head.

Suddenly, he would arrive in a small dusty village of straw-roofed mud huts, and a babbling crowd of near-naked people would appear. The sound of the noisy, giggling boys mingled with that of barking dogs and bleating goats. For those laboring in the fields, the word would quickly spread that 'the white god is here,' and all work would stop. My husband would seize the opportunity to preach to the crowds. He also kept their attention by singing songs like "A Little Child Shall Lead Them," and sometimes playing a 10-inch mouth organ and finally unstrapping a large wind-up phonograph and playing hymns on unwieldy 78 rpm records. The crowds would literally fight to put an ear close to the large horn out of which blared this "strange" music.

Every Monday, I would join Alf and "Dan-Juma" and we would visit a place called Tufa, about 6 miles from Izom. While cycling along the lonely road one day, we were suddenly confronted on the trail, by a number of huge red monkeys right in our path. I was frightened.

"Nan, ring your cycle bell," shouted Alf as he tried to stare out the monkeys."

The insistent sound did the trick and they dashed to the side of the road and climbed onto the rocks and peeped at us from their new vantage point.

We cycled as fast as we could and were soon away. No sign of the monkeys. What a relief! We arrived at Tufa and gathered the children to teach them and to hold a service. The three elder boys, Usuman, Galadima and Ungalu, had by now, built their own church. They had copied the one at Izom. Their chief helped them plan it. They were very proud of their achievement.

Mama always went with us to Tufa and helped with the language with the Bwaries who did not know the Hausa language that they were taught in the local school.

Black Magic

We remembered the day Mama's father died (he had been secretly visiting us for medicine and a chat). He was the head *Juju* (black magic) man and was afraid that natives might get to know of his secret visits to us. What would Mama do now? He being the eldest should take his fathers place and arrange the funeral as quickly as possible as a result of the heat. We had a time of prayer for him that God would give him strength to testify for the Lord. His younger brother arrived to ask us to come and hold a service at the graveside. Mama had sent him to us. They had built a hole under the house in which to bury the father in.

The body was wrapped in a mat. They put food and drink so that when the spirits moved on they would supposedly be refreshed. It was all strange to my husband and me. The *Juju* men were sitting on top of the earth that they had dug up. They looked so evil. They were waiting for us to finish our service to perform their own funeral rights. Then to our surprise we saw Usuman, Galadama and Ungalu, from Tufa. They had come to market to sell their goods 6 miles but had their Bibles and hymnbooks with them. They came to the funeral to testify that they were Christians. They sang Mama's favorite hymn, "There is a happy land, far, far, away...."

Then prayer followed by a message from Mama and my husband. It was most inspiring to hear Mama sing and speak on this sad occasion. He warned them "one day you will be as this corpse, decide now for Isa Almasihu (Jesus Christ) as Savior and be forever with Him in heaven or be cast away with Satan. Choose ye this day whom ye will serve."

Mama had such power at that moment and we closed with another hymn and benediction.

Mama had to remain to see to his father's things. My husband and I praised God for Mama's boldness in witnessing for Christ at this difficult time. Also for the witness of the boys from Tufa who were reading their Bibles in the market place.

I would often do battle with the local witch doctors who dispensed their evil magic. I had no qualms in approaching them about practicing their *juju* medicine on my patients —

111

something that was illegal under British colonial law. I had been called in several times by natives to try to save the lives of people who had been nearly killed off by the black magic of the witch doctors.

There were even occasions when Alf and I would be called to dig up new-born babies, who had been buried alive by the superstitious natives because the mothers had died in childbirth. The witch doctors had told the people that the evil spirit of the infant had caused the death of the mother and so the baby had to die, too.

Mama and Baba would watch in horror from behind a clump of trees for a burial to take place. They would hear the high-pitched shrieking of mourners, and watch the stiff, white-wrapped body of the dead mother being lowered into a freshly dug hole. Then the usually crying child, wrapped in a grass mat, was placed beside her, and the hole filled in.

When all was clear, they called us to dig up the suffocating child. If the mite was still alive, and most were, we would nurse them and then take them to the mission station at Diko that was run by fellow-missionary, Esther Anderson. There they had a large mission church and Christian women would foster the babies under the guidance of Esther. When they got older, these children who had been saved would be sent to a Christian orphanage and many of these babies eventually became nurses and evangelists.

Medical Work

Often while Alf was away, I would open the dispensary for the patients sitting under a large mango tree in front of a rectangular hut, and try to deal with the many medical problems of the area. Although I had only basic medical training, I was still expected to handle many difficult cases, and even at times was called to amputate gangrenous toes with kitchen scissors.

As the crowds lined up for treatment, Mama would preach to them. He would tell them about the love of Jesus and would often lead them in the singing of choruses. Even after being treated, the people did not want to leave. They enjoyed the time so much.

The medical work helped a great deal in gaining the confidence of the people. One day, I was called to see a boy in the village who had been stabbed by someone. I asked what had happened but they were afraid to tell the truth and said that he had fallen on a knife. But the wounds showed that he had been stabbed by someone else.

In a bid to kill the pain, I drugged him with generous doses of Aspirin, then cleansed the wound and bandaged it. This was done twice daily until it was healed. His grateful family gave us chickens and eggs in payment for the treatment.

On another occasion, an 8-year-old girl fell on a fire and was badly burned. Her parents had tried to treat her already by covering the burns with leaves, but when I examined it, I saw that her body was in a terrible mess. I cleaned it the best I could, but her chest was badly burned, as well as both arms and her back. I used special ointment and a lint jacket over the bandage. Three times daily this treatment was given until the wounds were healed and the child was well again.

A Double Healing

There was always much prayer about each case that I treated. The Lord did a work in their hearts through the healing of the body to the healing of the soul.

Nigeria was, at that time in 1941, still very much a British colony. But this was an area where not to many pith-helmeted civil servants and missionaries had previously ventured. It was a little too far from "civilization" to cope with.

But to Alf and me, it was heaven. Alf, especially, had blossomed as he had never done when he lived in the back-to-back terraced house in Liverpool's crumbling Toxteth district.

One day, during afternoon school, an appeal was made to follow Christ. Ungalu stood up and said, "I am going to follow the 'Jesus road' (hanya Yesu) and, as soon as he got to the door, he was taken by his people and punished. He was put into a little hut all by himself, but they forgot to confiscate his Bible, hymn book and his copy of *Pilgrim's Progress*, all of which gave him great comfort.

They said that he was to be a Pagan or a Moslem but should not follow "the white man's religion." The witch doctor treated him with his medicine. While he was in solitary confinement in the mud hut, he was given water that had been boiled from stewed leaves to drink. This was quite a common treatment used by these men of evil.

I went to see Ungalu a few days later and found him so happy. He said, "They put me in here to punish me but did not take my holy books away and I have been able to learn so much more of the Christian faith and nothing has harmed me". He was full of praise to the Lord for his goodness.

* * * * *

Alf became an unusual "judge" and was regularly called upon to adjudicate difficult disputes between natives. He would sit under the mango tree with most of the village for company and listen to the arguments. Then he would ask the Lord to give him Solomon's wisdom in giving the right judgment.

They called him *Mai hanjuri,* which means, "The patient one."

Surrounding the slight figure of my husband, wearing his white pith-helmet and khaki shorts, the crowds squatted silently in a semi-circle. "Dan-Juma" would gurgle contentedly in a swing-chair attached to the mango trees as Jumpa, his African playmate, pulled the rope to keep him moving so as to protect him from snakes and mosquitoes.

For us, the slithering snakes, monster rats, bitter-tasting quinine tablets, the tsetse flies constantly humming around our faces, the debilitating humidity, the hot air that clutched at us like a sauna, the inconvenience of having to constantly boil and filter the water, did not affect our unquestioning belief that God had called us to this remote area of West Africa.

Despite the difficulties, the peace we experienced was indescribable.

Chapter Fifteen

ALL AT SEA

Sadly, the happiness was soon to be broken. It began one night when Alf, normally in bed by 8:30 PM, had not arrived home by 9:30 PM. I was, by the meager light of a storm lamp, painting scrolls containing Scripture verses and hymns in the Hausa language. Just a stone's throw away, I could hear the ugly sounds of jackals and hyenas quarreling. Then I began to worry. It was then when I heard a rustle outside.

"I don't feel...."

Alf's word trailed off and he crashed head first onto the floor. He lay there, shaking, his face contorted in pain. I knelt down and took his temperature — it was 103 degrees Fahrenheit. Instinctively I rushed to the dispensary for medicine to bring the fever down but it was no use as he vomited it all back. I tried again but the same thing happened.

I tried to get him to bed but it was no good, he just fell on to the floor. In agony, he rolled from side to side, his pain-lined face streaming with sweat. His brown, curly hair, usually immaculately groomed, was lank and damp. He

117

gazed up at me with unseeing eyes. As I saw this, I recoiled in ill-concealed horror, but then I tried again to lift him and managed to lift his pain-racked body onto the bed, and covered him with a mosquito net. He lay in the pale flickering half-light, breathing harshly. His lips were pale.

I was not sure what to do next. My medical knowledge was minimal and we were many miles from the nearest hospital.

Dropping to my knees in desperation, I cried out in a voice that was barely audible, "Lord, I cannot face this yet, if it is Your will, then You will give me the strength for whatever lies ahead."

My face had been frozen with tension, but suddenly my mind became clear and I took a stick and a storm lamp and ventured through the dangerous and threatening bush to find the house boy, Ungalu's mud hut in the village, and I asked him to fetch Mama and ask him to travel to Abuja with a message to the District Commissioner.

Before Mama left on his desperate mission, he came and prayed for Alf. As he looked down at his flushed face, Mama cried out, "Lord, he that though lovest is sick."

Then I discovered that the bicycle he was to travel on had a puncture and I had to mend this and then pump the tire with air before Mama could set off.

While Mama was gone I changed the baby "Dan-Juma" (Daniel), washed him and got him ready for the road and journey to Minna. He was totally unaware of the life and death drama that was being played out at the time, and kicked his legs and gurgled contentedly.

After what seemed like an eternity, a truck driven by a Nigerian, arrived at the compound and I put in the back of it some folding chairs, a camp bed, a cot basket for the baby, and food for us all on the long journey to the hospital at Minna. Ungalu brought his roll-up bed and clothes as he was going with us.

Then Ungalu and the driver, lifted my husband on to the back of the open truck and gently laid him on the camp bed. I sat on a chair while Daniel was laid in a basket on the floor.

Along the way, the truck was forced to stop at a broken bridge which had to be rebuilt before we could continue. The driver went off to find his friends to get the necessary help and we were left on the truck sweltering in the heat of the day. However, we had plenty of food and water. We ate bananas and I gave the baby a bottle of milk.

My husband lay quiet. When the driver returned with his friends, Ungalu and I worked with them to build up the bridge that was broken so that we could cross. So began the drama that resulted in Alf's hospitalization. The doctor there discovered that he had the usually lethal combination of malaria, liver disorder and dysentery. The staff at Minna Hospital worked tirelessly to save his life, and after a week of treatment, he began to claw his way back to waking reality; to regain his strength, his very life.

I stayed at the language school for a few days until my husband was well enough to travel.

Soon we all returned to Izom and Alf gradually eased back into his routine as a missionary — visiting local tribes' people, taking Bible studies, and all the duties attached to mission work. For a few weeks he felt fine. Then the malaria returned. It was again followed by liver disorder and dysentery. Esther Anderson treated him at nearby Diko. The cruel tropics were exacting a terrible toll on him, yet manfully he struggled on, his emaciated featured and yellow skin, all pointing to the inevitable fact that Nigeria was no place for him.

We had both served five years in Nigeria and the time had come for a year's rest. Though what awaited us in war-ravaged British no one could tell.

"We Shall Fight on the
Seas and Oceans..."

Britain's Prime Minister, Winston Churchill, had announced about his country's plan to fight the Nazi's. He said, "*We shall fight on the seas and oceans... we shall never surrender.*"

We never really understand what these words would mean for us.

We were to spend over a year in England to recuperate then we would return to the work we loved at Izom. I packed eight boxes to be left behind for our return.

We were very sad to leave everyone but we also knew that they were in the Lord's hands. He would continue to lead them on. So we said good-bye and got on to the open lorry. We were all set for Minna, the two Tufa boys were there with Mama and Baba and the other boys from the school at Izom.

Tears welled up in our eyes as scores of our African "flock" gathered also outside the compound to say good-bye to us.

As we got into the back of the open truck, with our lives packed, lock, stock and barrel into boxes, the people held hands and sang, "God be with you tell we meet again."

The converts ran alongside the truck for at least a mile, waving and saying, "Return soon." The tears just kept flowing from them and us. It was the most moving experience of our lives. We really loved these people. We kept waving until they disappeared in a haze of dust that whirled behind the truck.

We waved and waved until they were out of sight. We had the usual tough journey, having breakdowns and mending bridges. We arrived at the language school at Minna in the early evening. Mr. and Mrs. Stewart greeted us with a nice cup of tea.

Mrs. Stewart had knitted a suit for Daniel to wear on the ship. She was aware that when the climate would change, it would be very cold. It was sweet of her to think of us as we had no warm clothes for him. He was now eighteen months old and was running about enjoying his own importance.

We spent another happy day of fellowship with these folks and then left for the two days journey to the Port of Lagos where we were to catch the ship to England.

After this long journey, we arrived at the dockside at Lagos, where we received a dire warning from a khaki-clad British civil servant.

"Mr. and Mrs. Wooding," he began with a grim expression on his face, "you may not make it to England. Boats are being sunk by the Germans all of the time. You are taking your lives in your hands by making the trip. Do you understand this?"

I nodded, holding Daniel in my arms, and said, "I have the choice of either my husband dying here, or of possibly making it to England and getting proper medical treatment for him. He won't last more than another few weeks here anyway. So we have no choice."

Everything was secret as the war was now raging just about everywhere. We would not know when we would sail until the last minute. We stayed one night in Lagos. The next day we went to board ship. I carried Daniel up the gang-plank of the Dutch passenger ship, *Stuvescent*, and was guided to our cabin by a steward.

Alf clutched a battered suitcase as he struggled bravely along behind us. A large trunk and several boxes containing our belongings were loaded in the hold by the African porters.

"There are ninety civilian passengers on the ship and the rest are soldiers," announced our Cockney steward. "We are to be part of a convoy of twenty-eight ships protected by four Royal Navy corvettes. "It's going to take a blinking miracle if we all make it back to good old Blighty."

It was a comfort to know that they were always on guard and on the look-out.

After he had left, Alf and I in the solitude of our cabin knelt down and asked for that miracle.

"Please God," Alf implored, "may we all make it safely to England. We hand our lives and that of our baby to You. We are completely in Your hands."

*   *   *   *   *

The sirens sent a chill of horror through most of those on board. Alf was about to start a funeral service that the captain had asked him to perform for an African passenger who had died of blackwater fever. We were just a couple of weeks at sea when the first German attack on our convoy came. Everyone had been instructed about what to do if we were hit.

"Get on the deck. Cut the rope from a lifeboat and take your children, but be prepared to jump into the water," said the weary captain, his voice shrill and strident.

"Why do we have to jump?" one woman, with two children clinging in fear to her skirt, asked in a desperate tone.

"Because, madam, you will have just one minute to get off the ship," the captain said. He paused, and then with acute embarrassment. added, "We haven't got enough lifeboats to go round. Most of us will have to end up in the sea."

I quickly harnessed our son into a tiny life-jacket and then strapped mine around my body. Alf also slipped into his life-jacket. For all ninety civilian passengers on our deck there was just one lifeboat. A member of the crew stood poised with a knife in his hand ready to cut the top that held that solitary boat. Who got in it was to be anybody's guess.

A huge explosion suddenly rocked the whole ship. Then came another and another. It had been as sudden as a cyclone appearing from a clear blue sky. Smoke began billowing from a vessel to the left and also from one in front. Distant screaming filtered through the smoke as hundreds of people leaped desperately from their stricken ships into the heaving Atlantic. There was utter pandemonium.

"Scatter! scatter!" an urgent voice bellowed from the loudspeaker system. We did scatter — like frightened sheep before a storm. Ships took off in different directions as the Royal Navy escort began the impossible task of fighting off the enemy and trying to rescue survivors from the angry sea. Hundreds drowned in a few terrible minutes.

Our ship shot off with another vessel and after four hours of apocalyptic horror, the captain sounded the "all clear" and announced that the Germans had retreated "for the time being" and we could all go to the dining room where a meal would be provided. It had been a frightening experience for all on board.

Only the engine crew were on duty, everybody else were on the different decks ready to jump at any moment.

After all that had happened, the people on board were not so frivolous as before since they were faced with shipwreck and death it had had a sobering effect on them.

I was sitting with the wives of some of the high officials. One of them, who was still shaking with fear, asked me, "Mrs. Wooding, how could you be so calm in all that we had gone through?" I told them some of my experiences with God.

"I know that He is real and He has never failed me since I learned to trust His Son, the Lord Jesus Christ. It can make all the difference when we trust Him as a child trusts its parents."

All through this, our baby son had been oblivious of the danger and was happily running around the deck and through the corridors.

That night brought another order. "Ladies and gentlemen," said the harassed purser, his face bleak, "it is not safe for any of you to sleep in your cabins tonight. I want all of the men to sleep in one of the saloons and the women and children in another."

Alf went to the purser. "Sir," he said in a low voice, "I know you will think that I am crazy, but I have committed this journey into the Lord's hands and I wish for myself and my family to sleep in the cabin."

The man looked in disbelief at the frail figure in front of him, and after a few moments of eye-to-eye dueling, said, "Do you realize that if we are hit, you will not have a chance?"

My husband nodded. "Yes, I know that. But I also know that we are God's hands."

As panic-stricken passengers tried to stave off the fear of death with large quantities of booze, the three of us slept soundly that night.

Next morning, a deputation of passengers came to Alf with a request. "Mr. Wooding, please hold an informal service for us," one of them said. He did this for the remainder of the hazardous journey and daily the room was packed to the doors.

For six nerve-racking weeks our convoy of two zigzagged its way from danger. Each morning, the passengers would rush to the deck to see if our companion ship was still there. Mercifully, it was. Normally the journey from Lagos to Liverpool took only fourteen days. This epic journey went on for forty-two days.

Daniel was, however, quite unaware of the dangers afloat. He would spend hours in the barber's shop sitting on the swivel chair turning around and around. The barber would also give him chocolate which he would nibble on. Then the soldiers would take him to the lower deck where they kept the monkeys they were taking back to Britain, and he would laugh at them as they ran around on their leashes.

Our little boy was also the life and joy of the crew. Whenever they were off duty they would come and plead to have Danny-boy and take him to the lower deck to talk to the parrot there.

The Liver Building

The sight of the towering Liver Building peeking out through the industrial haze of Liverpool's Pier Head brought a huge cheer from those on board the two ships.

I held Daniel close and shouted excitedly, "Danny boy, we're home at last. Thank God, we're home!"

I turned and noticed that Alf's eyes were brimming. He stood quietly thinking of how five years previously he had set sail to Nigeria, with such high hopes, from this very spot. Now he had returned a physical wreck — through still alive, just! It was by now early September of 1942.

Chapter Sixteen

HOME AGAIN

We were surprised that Liverpool was still stand ing. We had heard rumors, through the broadcasts of the infamous "Lord Haw Haw," the British traitor who had become a Nazi mouthpiece, that the port city lay in ruins through the bombing of the Luftwafe, but obviously this was a lie. Although some terrible damage had been inflicted on the city of my birth, most of it still stood proudly.

After clearing customs, we headed out towards the Pier Head where we caught an electric tram to Childwall. We were so used to being alone and shouting across the compound that we had an embarrassing experience.

Someone gave me a seat at the front of the tram. Alf, who was seated some way back, suddenly shouted out, "Cats home, boarders wanted." It was really funny and everyone had a good laugh. We learned to speak quieter after that.

We must have looked a strange couple to those on board, as we were wearing our summer clothes and it was now heading towards winter. Danny had a cream linen coat on, but his woolen suit that Mrs. Stewart made for him was under his coat.

We moved into the pebble-dash, semi-detached house in Okehampton Road, to live with my father, and my sister, Ethel.

The Beard

I was surprised to discover that my Dad now sported a fine white beard. He hugged me and said, as tears brimmed in his eyes, "Nancy, it's wonderful to have you home." He then hugged Alf, picked up our son, and held him aloft.

It was not long before he would sit Daniel on his lap and captivate him with his stories of 30 years with the Royal and Merchant Navy as salty as his personality.

Daniel would then take a deep breath and blow as hard as he could and his Granddad would pretend to fall into the chair. Then Danny would laugh because he thought he had blown him over.

Having been away five years, everything looked different and it took some time to adjust ourselves.

Ethel, who now worked at the Tate and Lyle sugar factory close to the River Mersey, moved out of her bedroom into the smaller one to make room for us.

One day, I visited my old home in Everton. I was shocked to see that much of the area had been flattened, and nothing was left of the old home and streets where I used to play.

I talked with someone on the street and heard the sad story how one dreadful night they were all in the bomb shelters.

"There was a wedding at one house on the terrace and they had left a light showing through," said a Mrs. Trainor, the lady I spoke with. "They had a bomb and the bridegroom was killed and the bride and her friends were taken to the hospital."

Mrs. Trainor went on to say that when the "all-clear" was sounded, she sent her son home to change his best clothes and to come right back.

"But no sooner had he gone, the sirens went off to warn of another raid," she told me. "His uncle went out to look for my boy, and they were never seen again. It was a terrible night for me."

I felt sad not to be able to see my friends again. I found the newspaper shop still there, and the owner, Miss Maddocks, and had a chat with her. She verified it all to be true about the bombing of Boyd Street.

I attended Donaldson Street Gospel Hall. It had now merged with another fellowship called Crete Hall. They had lost their hall in the bombing. I knew most of the Crete Street people. Some of them were my neighbors who used to play with me when I was a child.

Gradually, Alf's health improved. He had regular medical treatment at the Hospital for Tropical Diseases.

My husband and I had to take meetings for the SIM, sometimes for whole weekends. Because of the war, no lights were allowed, even on a bicycle. Consequently, it was difficult for him to find his way in the black darkness and so Alf would carry a hand torch.

One night, when he was on his own, he found that when he got off the train with his bicycle, he walked down the embankment and onto the tracks. Then, just before a train whizzed by, he managed to escape. A split second later and he would have been killed.

At this time, all food was rationed. When I went shopping I had to take a rationing book with me. Only so much allowed to each person. But it was enough for us. I enjoyed English food again. After only having African food it really tasted good.

The Birth of Ruth

It was September 1943. I was about to be delivered of my second baby. I had been home just twelve months. I went into the hospital on September 7 at 10:00 PM and, at midnight, Ruth was born. She was a lovely baby. A real joy to us.

Danny, her brother, who was nearly three years old was thrilled to have a baby sister. He would have someone to play with. "When will she grow big enough to play?" he asked one day.

The SIM decided we should return to Nigeria. But there were two problems: There were no ships available as D-Day was being planned and only troops and men urgently needed for the war effort were allowed to travel. Even more wrenching for us was that we would have to leave Danny behind and only take Ruth, who was nearly three months old.

Eventually, one space was available on a troop ship to Lagos and the SIM suggested that Alf could go, but not the rest of us. So my husband sailed back alone on a troop ship with the soldiers. Sleeping in a hammock, lining up for their meals and under the same discipline as the soldiers on board. It was quite an experience for him. He wrote telling me of his experience on board the troop ship.

As I had waved him off from the Pier Head, I was worried about him. He was still not too strong to deal with the tropical climate of Nigeria. I prayed that he would be all right. I cried a great deal after he had gone. The front room where we had spent time together alone reminded me of him. It would upset me not seeing my husband there. My father would call me as he knew that I was upset. I would wipe my eyes and come to him. He needed a lot of care, so I tried to help him. This helped me to forget at least for the time being.

* * * * *

Back in Nigeria, Alf felt the all-enveloping peace he had first experienced in the early days of his first term. He moved back to Izom to an ecstatic welcome from the natives there. Then, after a short stay, he moved on to Zaminaka. While there, an epidemic of meningitis swept through the area killing hundreds of people. He was seconded by the British Administration to travel among the natives handing out pills to try to fight the illness. As he traveled around the primitive villages he was bitten again and again by the tsetse fly and soon went down with sleeping sickness. That was followed by malaria and then dysentery. He began to shiver, sweat and vomit.

"Why, Lord," he questioned desperately, "should my missionary future be wrecked by all of this illness?" There was a pathetic misery in his voice.

He was treated by a missionary doctor who became more and more disturbed by his lack of physical progress.

"Why? Why? Why?" he kept asking the Lord. After more treatment, the attacks just continued and a bitter resentment began to seep into him.

This was compounded when Doctor Barnden, peering up from Alf's medical records, told him, "Mr. Wooding, you have no alternative but to leave the tropics for good. I'm terribly sorry."

Spidery Writing

Back in Liverpool, I became more and more concerned with each letter received from Alf. His spidery handwriting had become very difficult to decipher and I guessed the worst. He must be seriously ill again. Then they stopped coming altogether. I got in touch with the SIM headquarters in London and I was informed of his serious illness and that all of the 800 missionaries working in Africa were praying for his recovery. "There seems to be little hope, but with God all things are possible," I was told.

Time continued to drag by and then I got the news I had been dreading. It came from another missionary staying in Liverpool.

"Nancy," she said in a hushed voice, "I think you should prepare yourself for the fact that you will probably never see Alf again. We've had word that he's near to death. I am so sorry."

It was suggested that I should leave the children in a missionary home and go out to be with him as he was not expected to live (unless a miracle happened).

So I began to pack my boxes for Africa. Everything was secret as the war was still dragging on. I could hear anytime so I knew that I had better be prepared. SIM headquarters were able to book my passage as it was an emergency.

My sister Ethel stayed off work and went with me to Heighside, outside Manchester where I was to leave Danny at the Regions Beyond Missionary Union missionary home. Ruth, who was now nine months old, was to stay at Cousin Miriam's home. Danny liked the place and ran from room to room jumping excitedly on all of the beds. He liked Miss Rimmer, who was in charge of the facility.

My mind was in a daze as I tried to take care of last-minute arrangements. Clothes were on coupons and many other details had to be given. Ethel was to be guardian to the children and would be responsible for them during holidays and provide pocket money for them from time to time.

After we had agreed on the arrangements, it was time to return home. Miss Rimmer said, "You need not leave your son yet". So we were delighted to be taking Danny back with us. It was a very anxious time as we did not have any news of Alf. But headquarters let me know as much as they knew.

We were all together for Christmas, 1944, except for my husband. "Why doesn't Daddy come home?" Danny would often ask. I tried to explain the situation to him as best as I could.

I was expected to sail anytime now as all my papers were in order. I was longing to see Alf, but the parting with the children deeply concerned me. How could I face it?

The Only Hope

Just two days before I was due to leave, a knock came on the door. It was a telegram from an SIM leader in Nigeria, which said, "Don't sail. We have put Alf on a ship for England. It is the only hope for his recovery. All is secret so we are unable to tell you anymore. It will be a few weeks before you see him."

I did not know whether to laugh or cry. My father and sister were relieved to know that the children would not have to be parted from their parents. At least not for a long time.

Several weeks later I was taking a meeting at Calvary Church in Liverpool. It was a women's meeting that was 3:00 - 4:00 PM. I left Ruth in bed (now fifteen months old) and took Danny with me. Granddad said that he would look after Ruth until I returned from the meeting.

When I arrived back home there was my husband. Looking like a victim of the Belsen concentration camp, he had walked through the front door. When Ruth was roused from her bed, she was terrified of him. She had run in fear to her Grandfather, wondering who this skeletal figure was. He found it hard to believe that she had grown up in such a short time and now had such lovely curly brown hair.

I can still recall seeing this broken figure standing there, his hands outstretched for love. I ran to him and he swept me up in his arms.

I soon learned that the return journey had been as dangerous as the last. The big danger to him was now his terrible health. He was, as one doctor described him, a "museum of tropical diseases."

Chapter Seventeen

BIRMINGHAM BLUES

I have to say that my slight of stature husband — he was only five feet tall — was a battler and would not easily allow setbacks to ruin his life. The problems he had already encountered would be enough to floor most people, but he just kept getting up off the floor and starting again, believing that "all things do work together for good."

The next episode in his battle against illness, was fought out at Liverpool's Hospital for Tropical Diseases. He would spend two weeks in the hospital and then two at home. That difficult period went on for twelve long months, but then a doctor at the famous hospital told him the welcome news that he was clear of sleeping sickness and plans were again put in motion for our return to Africa.

But then came another knockout punch. Just as he was getting his life back together, another grievous blow greeted him. A cable arrived from Dr. Percy Barnden, the doctor who delivered our son in Vom, saying it would be "suicide" for Alf to return to Nigeria.

I watched in agony as he almost burst into tears. We both knew that the African odyssey was finally over. We would have to find a new sphere of service for the Lord.

I did my best to cheer him but had to say that we should face up to the fact that we would never see Mama, Ungalu, Baba, Usamen and Galadema again.

After I had finished my short, sad, monologue, Alf tried desperately to say that at least one of us should be on the mission field of Nigeria.

"Nan, why don't you go on your own and I'll stay here and look after the children," he offered one day. "You still have your health and ...."

"No, that wouldn't be right," I interrupted. "Danny and Ruth need both of us to take care of them."

I could see by my husband's face that he was relieved that I had made this decision, so we both began to pray about what should come next for us.

The Next Step

Around that time, a friend of Alf's had just left a church in Aintree and so he went to see him and his wife to find out how he was doing. The wife opened the door and told Alf that her husband was out.

Over a cup of tea, my husband shared with her the news about Nigeria and she suggested, "Alf, why don't you go to the meeting of the Barbican Mission to the Jews (now called Christian Witness to Israel) being held in a Liverpool church tonight. My husband will be there."

To the Jew First

She explained that the Reverend Isaac E. Davidson, a Polish Jew who now accepted Jesus as his Messiah, was to be the speaker.

"He is a great man of God and has founded the Barbican Mission to the Jews (Barbican is a area in London on the edge of city's financial district) and will be speaking about the need for Christians to preach the message of Christ to 'the Jew first.'"

So Alf took the bus over to the church and took his place among the large audience. As this man, with a distinctive mane of dark flowing hair, presented an inspiring message, Alf sat there enthralled.

After the powerful sermon, Alf decided to stay on to have a chat with the speaker. They immediately hit it off and Mr. Davidson obviously sensed my husband's love "for the lost." This initial conversation eventually resulted in Mr. Davidson inviting Alf to act as an evangelist to the large Jewish population of Birmingham, a city neither of us had ever visited before.

Several other jobs were being prayed over by us but the Lord seemed to confirm that Birmingham was to be our new home.

In hindsight, I am sure if we had known the shocks that were in store for us in those early days in England's second-city, we would never have gone there. But still God works in a "mysterious way."

Alf went on ahead to find accommodations for us. "I'll find somewhere nice for us to live," he had confidently told us as we waved him off at Lime Street Station. "When I've got that place, you can come and join me."

After several months, Alf finally called for us to join him.

The Journey South

Our spirits were sky high on that fateful day in late July, 1946, when we set off for our new life.

The furniture truck bumped relentlessly southwards with its sparse cargo of broken-down furniture and the three of us — Danny was by now five years old and Ruth was two

— on board. Our destination was Birmingham. As the ninety-mile journey progressed through smoke-caked towns like Crewe, Stafford and Wolverhampton, I led the children in the singing of Hausa choruses. By now I had taught them a whole selection of them and they knew them by heart. Our voices rose as we passed by factory smoke-stacks spewing black plumes into the air.

Alf had spent several months working in this bomb-flattened city with John Wolf, a Hebrew Christian, who had established a missionary work to the city's Jewish population — "God's chosen people" — many of whom had fled to the relative safety of England from the terrible "Holocaust" that had been taking place in Eastern Europe.

"I wonder what my bedroom will be like," Danny mused aloud.

"Will we have a nice garden, Mummy?" asked Ruth.

The large green furniture van weaved its way through Birmingham's Bull Ring shopping center. Danny pointed to the colorful stalls lining the steep cobbled hill that led precariously down from the Bull Ring into Digbeth.

As we drove towards the south of Birmingham I noticed that the city bore terrible scars of war. Everywhere I saw scenes of devastation. Whole streets lay in ruins. Factories, which had once been great, were reduced to rubble and twisted metal. World War II was now well over, but its black scars were there for all to see. There were 2,241 killed in the bombing of Birmingham. Many of the survivors would never recover from the mental scars of Hitler's Luftwaffe blitz.

Although large portions of Birmingham had been obliterated by the constant bombing, the area we were now in, Balsall Heath, seemed even more run-down and depressing than others we had passed through.

I began to feel bitterly disappointed as we pressed on through this dismal area.

"Brighton Road, Balsall Heath. Is that where we have to go?" the driver asked me as we all huddled together in the front seat of the truck.

"Yes, that's right; it's number ten." I squinted at the letter that Alf had sent which had the address on it.

A Huge, Ugly Face

I could see that the cloth-capped driver was just as taken aback as we were, as he drew up outside a large and extremely drab house which loomed over us like a huge ugly face.

A sick, sinking feeling began to rise in my stomach, as I knocked at the front door. A woman soon emerged with a cigarette hanging limply from her lips, and sporting a mass of plastic curlers.

"I've got no rooms to let at the moment," she barked. "You'd better clear off."

"No, I'm Mrs. Wooding. I understand my husband has arranged accommodation for us."

"Oh, that's right." she muttered, flicking burning gray ash onto the doorstep. "You've got the attic and another room. You'll have to share the bathroom with someone else though."

Mrs. Reid, a war widow, explained that Mr. Wooding had gone out for the day with Mr. Wolf on a Sunday school outing to Weston-super-Mare. It was by now late afternoon and she said that she expected him back "at any moment."

"I think you should all come in and have a cup of tea, and then I'll show you your rooms," she said magnanimously.

We all trooped into her ground-floor lounge and were introduced to Mr. Mohammed. His thin lips were pulled into a smile that lit up his swarthy face, showing very small, very yellow teeth.

"He's my special lodger," she explained, exchanging a grin with her greasy friend. "He helps keep my spirits up in these terrible times."

The tea arrived and, as we sipped the revolting liquid, Alf arrived breathlessly with Mr. Wolf, a dark-skinned man. Obviously flustered, my husband was full of apologies for being late.

Mr. Wolf patted Danny on the head, then he suddenly lunged at my son. "Now, little Danny, I want to kiss you on the cheek." His eyes narrowed. My son recoiled in fright. He obviously wondered who this strange figure was who was bending over him.

"Why should I let you kiss me?" little Danny asked defiantly.

Kissed by a Wolf

"Because I want you one day to tell your grandchildren that you have been kissed by a wolf ...." With that he kissed Danny on the cheek and threw back his head and roared with strange laughter.

It was now time to view our lodgings. As we made our way up the uncarpeted stairs that ascended into the shadows, Alf caught the disappointment in my face.

"I'm sorry, Nan," he said, "but I have tramped the streets for weeks trying to get something and this was the only place I could find that would take children. Things are dreadful here. There is just no accommodation for couples with families."

On his meager wage of three pounds (six dollars) a week, Alf had found life in post-war Birmingham, tough beyond words. Whole areas had been wiped out by Hitler's incessant bombing raids. In sheer desperation, he had finally settled for this seedy house in Birmingham's "red light" district.

The accommodation was absolutely terrible. It was no more than a couple of dingy rooms. Mrs. Reid took out a match and lit the gas lamps in the "living room" and "bedroom" that Alf and I would share.

I stared in horror in the gloomy, flickering light, at the state of our accommodation as the smell of decay and rot reached my nostrils.

In the main "living room" bugs scuttled up and down the mildewed wallpaper while a few cockroaches fled across the floor, bare of carpet. A dank piece of flowered linoleum that had probably been in the same place for twenty years, was all that lay between the floorboards and our shoes.

Aesthetics had a low priority in our new home.

"Alf," I finally exploded, "this place doesn't even have electricity. It isn't fit for an animal, let alone a family."

"I'm sorry, Nan, but it's the best I could get." He kept repeating that he was "so sorry."

I fought back the tears of anger as I discovered the dingy place didn't even have a cooker

"Come on, Mrs. Wooding. it's not all bad," said Mrs. Reid brightly, as she discharged more ash onto the floor. "There is one problem, however. We have only one gas meter for the whole house. You'd probably be better off using candles."

She paused to take another puff on her cigarette and allowed it to curl into the recesses of her lungs before blowing it out and continuing. "The rent is very reasonable. Only twenty-seven shillings a week."

"But that will hardly leave us enough to live on," I protested.

The landlady's mouth twitched.

"Take it or leave it, Mrs. Wooding."

Mrs. Reid was certainly a venomous creature who could turn and sting at the slightest provocation.

On that first night Ruth and Danny couldn't sleep. The noise of slurred singing from The Malt Shovel, a pub across the road wafted through their window. Suddenly there came the urgent ringing of a police siren. It got louder and louder and was followed by a squeal of brakes.

"It's the cops," Danny yelled excitedly as Ruth lay cowering under the blankets.

"Let's have a look and see what's happening!"

Tide of Hate

He pressed his nose to the dirty window pane and saw in the dim glow of the moon and nearby streetlight, two women fighting with each other outside the pub. A group of policemen were vainly trying to separate them as they flailed away at each other. Without warning, the spitting combatants suddenly turned on the police and attacked them. Helmets flew as the men in blue tried to stem the scratching tide of hate.

Things got worse when the pub doors shot open and out poured a group of male drinkers who had decided to come to the aid of the women.

"Come on Ruth," Danny said hoarsely. "Don't be a scare-baby. Come and watch this. It's really exciting."

By now Ruth was sobbing in sheer terror. She put her hands tightly over her ears, then hid her face under the pillow.

"It's getting better. There are more police running down the road. Look, there's a Black Maria coming as well. There's about twenty people fighting with the police, but they're winning and pushing them into the van."

Finally her innocent blue eyes peeked out at her brother and they almost got the giggles.

For nearly three-and-a-half years those nightly fights inside and outside The Malt Shovel kept him glued to that attic window. It became such a regular occurrence that Danny didn't wait for the police to arrive. He knew that as soon as "chucking out" time came, trouble was on its way.

I remember on the first night that Alf and I knelt on the bare floor and prayed fervently. We asked the Lord to give us grace to bear our conditions. I'll be honest. I couldn't see any light ahead at the time. It seemed to me to be far worse than anything I had encountered in Nigeria.

Looking back now, however, I know God knew best and moved us to Birmingham for a reason.

Chapter Eighteen

THE BIG "C"

When I got over the initial shock of my new home, I discovered that most of the residents of the house were involved in a variety of criminal activities. Many had false names because they were on the run from the police.

At first, I found Birmingham more difficult to cope with than Nigeria. The natives in Africa were far more responsive to the gospel and really seemed to love us.

Mind you, the Brummies had just been through a terrible war and life was hard. That included rationing of food and clothing. It was a struggle for everyone to keep body and soul together.

Besides trying to find rooms for us, Alf had been busy starting up a youth club in the nearby Clifton Road school. It was already being attended by some 160 children. He also had a thriving Sunday School there, and had established, with the help of Mr. Wolf, a little Sunday night service in a rented room at the Cooperative Halls on Stratford Road, Sparkhill.

To try and keep their minds off the violence, Alf and I arranged for Danny and Ruth to take piano lessons with Mrs. Helen Price, and also attend missionary rallies at Tennessee, a huge house in the Moseley district, hosted by Mrs. Helen Alexander-Dixon, who when she was Helen Cadbury, of the famous chocolate family, founded the Pocket Testament League. These were times of contrast for us all. Her home was magnificent, as were the grounds, while our home was absolutely terrible.

Our accommodation was a constant source of embarrassment to me. I was used to better things.

What made things worse was the fact that the police often stood across the road from the house and took note of everyone who came in and out. Alf, who had by now been ordained as a pastor and wore a "dog collar," was probably also under suspicion. The police probably thought he was a bogus priest.

One day my father and sister Ethel came from Liverpool to stay with us. As they went up the steps, the officers ran across the road and stopped them. They questioned them for several minutes for their reason for visiting the house. They obviously felt that they were up to no good.

Afterwards, my father asked pointedly, "Anne, why are living in such a dump?"

What could I say to him except, "This is where God has placed us as a family."

* * * * *

I soon came to realize the impact my husband had made in our local area in the short time he had been there. On my first Sunday, as I approached the Clifton Road school for the Sunday School meeting, I was stopped by a gnarled faced old lady with dark hair, who looked every inch a gypsy.

"Are you the little minister's wife"? she asked.

"Yes," I replied rather taken aback.

"Well, I'd like to shake your hand. He has saved my life," she said.

I found out from her that Alf had been visiting door-to-door in the area in a bid to get parents to send their children to the newly formed Sunday School. Not realizing the drama going on inside, he had knocked on her door. Old Emma, as we later called her, was trying to commit suicide when she heard the urgent rapping.

She was old, depressed and sad. Life seemed so pointless to her. She had been sitting in front of her old gas fire with the unlit jets full on. If Alf had knocked seconds later she would have died.

That knock on the door jolted her and she quickly turned off the gas and staggered to see who was there.

"I am sorry to bother you, but I wondered if you would send your children to the Sunday School we have just started in the school next door," said Alf.

"Children, I've no children" she declared in disbelief at his request. "But I'll tell you something. God has sent you here today. He sent you to stop me from gassing myself."

Alf was stunned at her admission. Emma invited him into her little terraced home and confessed to him what she had tried to do. She further surprised him by asking, "Do you preach Christ crucified for our sins"?

Still speechless, Alf nodded his head. After a long chat, the old lady prayed with Alf and promised she would never attempt such a thing again.

When I heard this story I realized that although we had a long struggle ahead of us, God had real plans for us in this city.

Emma soon became a regular at our Sunday services and often helped us out during the severe coal shortage of those days. We didn't even possess a radio then and so once a week, she would invite us to listen to the hit "ITMA" (It's That Man Again) show with Tommy Hanley.

Soon Alf and I had a thriving work both at Clifton Road School and in the Cooperative Hall. Alf's door-to-door visits had produced a congregation of Christians who worshipped with us each week.

One amusing experience took place at the Cooperative Hall that nearly wrecked our evening service and reduced the congregation to a state of helpless laughter.

Cat and Mouse

Alf launched into a long-winded prayer. As he did, a cat dashed into the hall, chasing a helpless little mouse. One by one the congregation noticed what was happening and terrified, they lifted their legs in the air. None of them wanted the darting mouse running over their feet. Eventually, when Alf finished his prayer, he opened his eyes and was shocked to see virtually the whole congregation with their legs in the air. The mouse had, by then, disappeared - down the cat's mouth. But everyone still had their feet pointing upwards.

He smiled and then hilarious pandemonium broke loose.

Financial Struggle

During those first few years it was a real struggle to make ends meet financially. I was forced to take a job serving behind the counter in a cafe at Swanshurst Park, Acocks Green, about six miles from our home. Alf used to come to the park during the week for his meals there. Often he would hand out tracts to visitors to the cafe.

Sometimes a Jewish person would come in and Alf would take the opportunity to talk to them about the Messiah. The children would join us after school walking the long trek of about a mile to the nearest bus stop that would bring them to the park.

* * * * *

I could tell that Alf was excited.

"It looks like we've got our own mission hall," he beamed.

"Well, Alf, that's wonderful," I enthused.

"It seems," he continued, "that the minister of the Sparkbrook Mission in Alfred Street. has had to leave Birmingham. His wife is ill and needs to move to a better climate.. He wants us to take over the place."

At last Alf had his own church. After consultations with Barbican headquarters in Chislehurst, Kent, we got the go ahead to have the place and now we had a permanent center for our work. Of course, this made a tremendous difference to us. There are always difficulties in hiring halls and school rooms.

Soon we held a district-wide campaign where we knocked on doors and invited people to the meetings in the wooden mission hall and, among those converted to the Lord Jesus Christ, were two school girls who later became two of our most valued workers, Margaret Swift and Sheila Belcher.

In a short time we had a thriving congregation and formed an evangelistic team which visited other churches. They included Cyril Price, a Welsh-born school teacher who had a fine rich tenor singing voice; his wife Helen, a music teacher and pianist; Mr. and Mrs. Judkins; Miss Elsie Budd and Miss Kath Welsh, who went on to become the matron of an old peoples home in Birmingham.

One Saturday evening we held a service at Acocks Green Mission and that night a soldier in uniform, Dennis Stevens, came in. He formed a friendship with Margaret Swift and they were later married by Alf at our church. Dennis and Margaret eventually went to Nigeria to work with the SIM.

Another of our members, Harry Poole went to Nigeria and did some wonderful medical work there along with his lovely wife, Joan. Both he and his family were in Nigeria right through the bloody Biafran civil war.

Although we were encouraged by the leap forward in our work we were still living in our rooms in Balsall Heath. We had almost given up hope of ever buying a home for ourselves. Through my work at the cafe I had managed to save what to us was the huge amount of 200 pounds and we had high hopes of that being enough for a deposit on a house. But when we inquired about a mortgage, the people at the Building Society (mortgage company) laughed in our face and said that "we hadn't a hope."

Again, as in all our crisis times in Birmingham, we turned to the Lord, and once again God heard our prayers in a way we could never have dreamed. Miss Moon, a wealthy Christian lady had heard about our plight. She said that she wanted to help us and, true to her word, she helped us buy a large comfortable house with a garden (something almost unknown to Daniel and Ruth), in Featherstone Road, Kings Heath

Work with the Jews

So far, I have only mentioned our work with the Gentile population of Birmingham. Our first concern, however, was always with the Jewish population in the city. They lived mainly in the pleasant Cannon Hill and Edgbaston areas of the city.

Alf spent much of his time drawing up lists, usually drawn from the telephone directory, of people with Jewish-sounding names, then visiting them. He would offer them a special prophesy edition of the New Testament and also try to talk to them about Christ.

Very rarely, as any Jewish worker will bear me out, did he receive a warm welcome. One day Alf was fortunate to escape with his life. He walked into a Kosher butcher's shop and everything went smoothly until he offered the Jewish butcher a piece of Christian literature.

The angry meat dresser picked up the meat axe and yelled at my terrified husband.

"If you are not out of here immediately I'll make mince-meat of you," he yelled angrily.

Alf did not wait to see if he meant it!

Regularly, during his visiting, he had doors slammed in his face - an occupational hazard of all Jewish missionaries. But occasionally he was invited into their homes to talk and even, at times, was allowed to pray with them.

One day Alf, visiting in Sparkbrook, handed out a tract to a Jewess called Mrs. Abraham. She surprisingly invited him to her home and revealed that her husband had left months previously because their son had become a Christian and she had refused to condemn him for it. She told Alf of the deep loneliness and confusion she felt.

Soon, Mrs. Abraham was regularly attending our Sunday evening services, that was while we were still at the Cooperative Hall and she said how she greatly enjoyed hearing about the Jewish heroes of the Old Testament. She was particularly impressed when she heard the then Barbican Director, The Reverend I.E. Davidson (himself a converted Jew), speak at the Birmingham annual meeting of the mission.

Sadly, when we moved to our new Mission Hall, she refused to come because she did not want to be seen going into it by her Jewish friends.

"The Cooperative Hall is a public building and so if people see me going there it doesn't matter", she explained. "But the mission is a church and that could bring me big problems."

Because of this we lost contact with Mrs. Abraham for several years. Eventually we met up again one day while I was out shopping. Mrs. Abraham appeared to be delighted to see me again and promised to come to our Wednesday women's meeting.

However, she still refused to attend on Sunday. During one of her visits to the women's meeting, she accepted Jesus Christ into her life as her Lord and Messiah. We were allowed to visit her husband and soon they both agreed to join us at our Sunday evening services.

One day we received a letter from their son (a missionary in North Africa) thanking us for our 'kindness' to his parents. He said he was praying for his father's conversion.

Then Mrs. Abraham died and Alf was asked to conduct her funeral service at the mission center. All her family attended. Alf also led the committal ceremony at the cemetery.

A few months went by and Mr. Abraham was taken ill and so we visited him regularly at his home. We prayed with him and read the scriptures. We were sure that through this he finally committed his life over to the Messiah and are confident one day this family will be in heaven.

The Abraham's story, though, was rare in those days. It was many years before the Messianic revival swept through the American Jewish community. Then, there were not many Jews who came to Christ. The cost was too high.

Often Alf would receive back prophecy edition New Testaments given previously to a Jew. with bad things like "Jesus Christ was illegitimate" written in the fly-leaf. This naturally upset us both.

Often Alf would take a group of students from the Birmingham Bible Institute on tours of local synagogues. This of course, had to be previously cleared with the Rabbi. On one occasion Alf was able to present a Rabbi with a copy of a Christian book on doctrine called "In Understanding Be Men."

On one occasion a group of students (with my husband) knocked on the door of the Chief Rabbi of Birmingham's home. They had not realized he lived there and were rather taken aback when he interrupted their first few words with, "Do you know who I am? I am the Chief Rabbi. Do you think you can convert me? We have our scriptures and worship, so go to the Christians. They will hear you.". With that he slammed the door.

The Crisis

During this time a real crisis hit our family. Over the years since his tropical illnesses, Alf had been growing gradually weaker. One Sunday morning in 1961 he collapsed in the pulpit of the Sparkbrook Mission.

To make things worse for us, Daniel, in his teens, had left home to live in Toronto, Canada. He said he wanted to make a new life, though in reality he later confessed that he was in total rebellion against God.

I had continued to write to him and one day I had to share with him the news that his father had colon cancer and had probably only a few months to live.

"Please come home and say 'good-bye' to your father," I said in one letter, which was probably the most difficult I had ever written.

After a year he came home by liner from Montreal and, along with Ethel, I met him at the Pier Head in Liverpool. He was shattered, as we all were to hear that his father had cancer.

We all went to see Alf at the Queen Elizabeth Hospital in Birmingham and Danny broke down as he saw his father again looking like a victim of a German concentration camp.

When we got back to our home, I gathered my children together and asked them to join with me in prayer for God to spare Alf's life.

"I can't pray," said Danny, his voice choked with emotion. "I don't know the Lord."

"You know how you can know Him," I told him.

With that, he left Ruth, who had already made her decision for Christ, and went up to his bedroom. He sank to his knees and poured out his heart before the Lord.

"God, I ask you to please forgive me for my anger towards you and my parents," he began in high, strangled voice. "Now I want you to please come into my life and use me for Your service."

With that, he emerged in the room, his face covered in tears, and we all prayed for the dangerous surgery that was to take place the following morning.

We had no phone in the house and so next day, we all trooped down to the nearest pay-phone which was located on Alcester Road. Nervously I dialed the number and was soon connected with the sister on the cancer recovery ward.

"Mrs. Wooding," the lady told me, "he's come through the operation really well and is now recovering. Why don't you come and see him later this afternoon?"

Alf looked terribly ill when we arrived at the ward. He had undergone a successful illiostomy operation, which had saved his life.

His face lit up when Daniel told him of his conversion. "That has made all my illness worthwhile," he whispered.

When I first came to Birmingham, I thought God had made a dreadful mistake. Things at the time couldn't have been worse. Now I realize that God's plans are always best. After reading this I am sure you will agree.

THE EPILOGUE

Daniel eventually married Norma, a beautiful raven-haired young lady from the Aston district of Birmingham, and they had two wonderful sons, Andrew and Peter, who continued the Wooding family tradition working as missionaries in various countries, including Denmark, Poland and Tanzania, with Youth With A Mission.

Daniel has since become an international journalist and went on to work with a series of newspapers in London, including the *Christian*, the *Sunday People* and the *Sunday Mirror*, and is now a commentator and correspondent with the UPI Radio Network in Washington, DC. He also is a syndicated columnist

Before his long journalistic career, he and Norma, along with Ruth, started The Messengers, an evangelistic outreach team that made a big impact on Birmingham. They took the message of Christ out to coffee-bars, public houses and open air. Regularly 50 young people would squeeze into Daniel's flat at Featherstone Road for weekly Bible study and prayer.

Then they moved into the needy and heartbreaking field of drug addiction and, along with a group of Birmingham ministers and clergymen founded Europe's first ever drug rehabilitation farm at Hill Farm in Alvechurch, Worcestershire.

His first book, *Junkies Are People Too*, was published by Scripture Union, and told the story of Hill Farm.

One of the people he introduced to the work with drug addicts, Walter Moore, went on to found Addulam Homes, which now is doing a tremendous work with the homeless of the United Kingdom.

After many years in Fleet Street, Daniel — he now calls himself Dan — and his family emigrated to the United States of America on June 28, 1982, and, along with Norma, runs a ministry called ASSIST (Aid to Special Saints in Strategic Times,) which is based in Garden Grove, California. This work is, at present, helping to disciple some 610,000 new Christians in the former Soviet Union, as well as running a sister-church program with congregations in Cuba, Nicaragua and Romania. Dan is also the author of some thirty books.

Andrew returned to the UK and is the author of five books and the editor of a Christian comic book called *Plus*, based in Worthing, Sussex. He is also involved with the youth work of his church.

Peter has married a lovely girl called Sharon and they have produced my first great-grandchild, Sarah Emma Wooding, who was born in November, 1994. They all live in North Wales and he now edits a church publication and is a youth leader at his church.

Ruth has married Allen Ross, who is Aunt Lottie's grandson, and has taught for years in a school on the outskirts of Liverpool. She, like myself, also attended Redcliffe Missionary Training College in Chiswick and is deeply involved in Christian work at her local church.

We came to the end of our Mission Hall work and we handed over the buildings to a West Indian group. They have since built a lovely brick sanctuary on the site.

Alf and I retired to a Christian community in Essex, and then settled in sheltered accommodations in Wallasey, Cheshire.

Sadly, in March of 1994, at the age of eight-three, Alf passed away. It was a few months before Sarah Emma was born. He had survived the trauma of his tropical diseases, cancer, and then Parkinson's disease, for many years.

I am now registered as partially sighted. But I know that God still has much in store for me. I still work amongst the blind through the Torch Trust for the Blind.

I look back at our exciting adventure with God and can see God's hand through it all. We had two couples — the Stevens and Pooles — follow in our footsteps to Nigeria with SIM.

We saw young people like Peter Conlan go on to serve the Lord with Operation Mobilization around the world. We saw John and Grace Miles go on to start a mission to Eastern Europe and Africa called REAP International. This couple even bought our home in Featherstone Road, where they still live at the time of writing.

For me, it has been an exciting adventure with God — a life of **BLIND FAITH**! Will you join me in this great venture?

ASSIST (Aid to Special Saints in Strategic Times) is a ministry that links people together around the world for friendship, evangelism and discipleship. It has pen pal ministries between people in the West and those in the former Soviet Union and Romania. It also is conducting Project Disciple Russia, which is placing discipleship materials in the hands of 610,000 new Christians in the former USSR.

The ministry also has humanitarian and literature efforts to Nicaragua, Cuba, Romania, Bulgaria and the former Soviet Union.

A Sister church program also is being conducted between churches in the West and those in Cuba, Nicaragua and Romania.

For details and for other books available from ASSIST, contact your nearest ASSIST office:

ASSIST USA
PO Box 2126
Garden Grove
CA 92642-2126
USA

ASSIST Europe
PO Box 789
Sutton Coldfield
West Midlands B74 2XJ
ENGLAND

ASSIST Canada
PO Box 483
Woodstock
ONT. N4S 7YS
CANADA

ASSIST New Zealand
1 Burton Place
Flaxmere
Hastings
NEW ZEALAND